if these Tables could Talk!

Worthy Tales from Soup to Nuts

by Linda Hepworth

To Lauren —

Best wishes

Linda Hepworth.

Edited by Carol Callahan

ISBN: 145648172X

Back cover photo by T. Nyhuus

TABLE OF CONTENTS

ACKNOWLEDGEMENTS

There are so many people who have helped me with this project. First, Thor, my partner and best friend, who supported me from the beginning, fed me and took care of all the day to day chores while I spent my time writing. I want to thank my family for being my guinea pigs, listening to my stories and jokes, and my Mom for instilling a love for the English language in me. Next, my editor, Carol Callahan, for her professionalism, computer skills, and assistance in bringing a loose collection of stories into a coherent concept. Many thanks to "Mary Futon" Hughes, my Marketing Director, for website design, hosting my book launch parties and generously donating a computer. I'm also grateful to all my friends for their optimism and belief in me. I wish to thank my managers over the years who allowed me to be myself. Lastly, I wholeheartedly thank the customers who opened up their hearts and made my experiences so memorable.

NOTES ON THE ILLUSTRATIONS

Most of the illustrations in this book are actually decorative collar pins that I have accumulated over the years. I've acquired a reputation for wearing them. They uniquely decorate my uniform and signify seasons and occasions. My customers like to check which one I will have on for any particular day. Many of these pins came from my customers; others came from friends and family. All are illustrative of my journey through my career.

CHAPTER ONE

Let's Go To Work!

Let's Go To Work

As a waitress, my first priority is to see that the customers enjoy themselves. The food has to be good, what they asked for, and served in a timely fashion. But the exceptional experience in a restaurant depends on the service. I make the connection between the kitchen and the dining room.

Customers can be neighbors, friends or travelers. They come in all shapes, sizes and moods. I'm anxious for you to read on and meet some of my favorite customers, and hear their tales.

Put up your hair, slip on some comfortable shoes, and stride with me from behind the counter, under the tables, up to the seats at the bar. We're going to work!

Neighbor Notes

One of our neighbors always stopped in at the restaurant for a drink on his way home from work. He was quite literally a regular, being on the same schedule for years. He liked to sit in the same spot, have a drink, see his friends, and then go home for dinner. If work kept him overtime and he showed up later than usual, I always teased him about being late for his shift.

One evening, hours after he had gone home, I spied our neighbor sitting at the bar. He was even sitting at a different seat, being a later hour and a different crowd than he was used to. I told him that it was good to see him, but a little unusual, and asked what brought him there at that time of the evening. He made everyone laugh when he answered, "Someone left my gate open, and I wandered out!"

Patio Wildlife

A 6-year-old boy enjoyed sitting outside on the patio when he came to our restaurant. He liked to feed snails some of his lettuce, and always looked for them in the foliage before he chose his table to sit down. He thought it was always the same snail, and so was looking for 'his' snail.

After he finished his salad and the snail had something to munch on, I brought the little boy a small steak. I noticed that he was having trouble cutting it with his steak knife, so I offered to cut it for him. As I was cutting, I got to the end with the small crispy fat. He said, "Ugh! Fat!" I realized he didn't like that part, so I put it aside. Then without thinking, I reached over, popped the crispy fat into my mouth and ate it. He was astonished! I guess I was trying to show him that it was quite good and it wasn't going to kill him.

When I realized what I had done, I told him that a waitress really should not eat a customer's food, so I reached into my pocket and handed him a quarter. His Mom was watching all of this and just smiling throughout.

Some time went by, and besides the snails, there were yellow jackets buzzing about to enhance the wildlife experience of the patio. One was really bothering my little friend. Yellow jackets are carnivorous, and seem to enjoy our patio quite a bit. I took a napkin and whacked the yellow jacket. It dropped to the ground, then I stepped on it. The little boy said, "Thank you" and handed my quarter back to me.

Working with Bugs

As a waitress, you have to be quick on your feet, especially when confronted with insects. Insects usually come in with the salad and produce boxes. The cooks wash the vegetables and lettuce in a big sink filled with water. The lettuce is then spun in a large salad spinner to remove the water. Well, sometimes those pesky insects are tenacious and are still clinging to the salad when it is served.

I remember one particular grasshopper that climbed out of the salad at the table. It crawled onto the side of the plate and shook itself off. The customer was horrified. I carefully removed the grasshopper from the customer's plate, and took the poor thing outside after his bath.

Another time, when a green inchworm suddenly found itself on a shocked vegetarian's fork, I quipped, "At least it's organic!"

We try really hard in the restaurant to keep everything clean and presentable. When I put myself in the position of the customer and consider their feelings and reactions, I realize that I may have been too cavalier in these situations. But they are after all unavoidable. I feel sorry for the small creatures that find themselves in rather unpleasant circumstances.

Irate Customer

Most of our customers are fabulous people, are a pleasure to serve and have even become friends. Sometimes they're not.

We were very busy one night, running around, with customers waiting. Even the boss was helping: seating people, bringing their bread, water, cocktails. I went up to a table with a man and a woman, he with a black leather jacket and a black leathered look on his face. I said, "Good evening" and he bellowed, "No one's been to our table!" So I answered back, "Then how did you get your bread and water?" His table was one of the tables that the boss had been to, and I could clearly see that he had brought them the bread and water. The unhappy customer did not like my flip answer. I patiently took their order, but I was uncomfortable. He was uncomfortable.

I don't remember much about the woman who was with this 'gentleman' because she didn't say much. They both ordered meals which came with soup and salad. I brought a tureen of soup to the table. When it came time to serve his soup, the irate customer made me so nervous that my hands were shaking. I didn't want him to see that he had 'gotten' to me, so I put the tureen down and instead of ladling the soup, told them to help themselves. At this, he stood up and yelled, "Now she's refusing to serve me!" Unfortunately, this was true.

Things were going from bad to worse. The entire restaurant heard what was going on, including four women sitting at a neighboring table, which was by the outside window. I went to the boss and said that I was having trouble with table #5. The boss told me not to worry, he had noticed that the customer had come in with a bad attitude, and not to let it bother me.

A little later on, this irate man and his companion had received their dinners and were eating, when the man decided to leave NOW! He stood up from his table and loudly proclaimed that they wanted to have their check and get out of our restaurant. So with my shaky hands, I scribbled out the check, as he came from the table and was waiting by the front door to pay. His poor dinner companion was still sitting at the table trying to finish her meal.

The boss kept a close eye on the situation. The irate customer threw the money at me, just enough for the bill which didn't surprise me. I wasn't expecting much of a tip. The man stepped out onto the patio, still fuming and pacing, to wait for his dinner companion.

Just then, the four women seated nearby, tapped the window lightly until the unhappy customer looked up. Then all four of them threw him the bird! Just like that! Four little middle fingers all standing straight up like little soldiers! And the boss laughed, "Did you see that?"

The good news is everybody had seen that, including the unhappy customer who scurried off never to be seen again.

I thanked the ladies who said, "Honey, are you alright?" Everyone else was very sympathetic, and my hands finally stopped shaking. You can't please everybody.

FEELING AT HOME

One night, a single man came in for dinner. He told us repeatedly how delicious the dinner was and how happy he was to have found such a good restaurant. He introduced himself to me and asked if he could meet the chef.

I escorted him into the kitchen and he complimented the chef on the dinner. He said that he traveled a lot and was experienced in dining out. Ours was the best meal he had eaten in quite some time. He gave the chef his business card, and went back to his table to enjoy his dessert. Then he got up and left without paying for his dinner!

We used the information on his business card and called him. He apologized profusely and returned promptly to the restaurant, where he paid the bill with a nice tip for me. His explanation was heartfelt and cute. He said it was because he had felt so much at home!

My Day Off

A particular day off remains etched in my mind. My man and I were invited to the house of a friend of a friend for supper. Not knowing our hosts well, we put together a beautiful salad, meant to impress: fresh lettuce from the farmer's market, lovely tomatoes, artichoke hearts, plus a homemade dressing that we were proud to share.

The home was a secluded cottage nestled up in the hills of Fairfax. We had never been there before and the instructions were complicated, so much so that our host drove down the mountain to meet us in town and escort us up. The hills of Fairfax are a maze of single lane, twisted roads, and clogged with parked cars. As we drove up, we were discussing what a problem it would be to escape quickly in an emergency. We learned later that there used to be a funicular built into the hillside to facilitate grocery shopping and transport. Now everyone depended on cars, and there were a lot of them.

All told, there were six of us for dinner: the host, his wife, my partner and myself, another man, and my friend. The men were all big people, and everyone at the party had hearty appetites. The host was preparing steaks, and beautiful steaks they were! He had six large, gorgeous T-Bones sizzling on the grill. There were also two very large black dogs on the back deck lounging around. I like dogs and these were friendly, so I played with them while we were waiting for dinner.

While our host presided over the grill, we sat on the deck that overlooked Mt. Tamalpais. What a view! I knew then why people put up with the difficulties to live there. It was serene, cool on a hot summer evening, just lovely, really. I was happy to be there, and glad that I had put an extra effort into my salad that I hoped would be well received.

Music was playing, the soft lights on the deck sent shadows into the trees, and we all sat down to a nice meal. Interestingly enough, I was the only one to eat all my steak. I am known to be a big eater, but that night I was particularly hungry. I looked around, and noticed to myself, that with these big guys here, I could out-eat them all. I sort of quietly puffed up with pride.

As we finished and started clearing the plates, the host got the dog's bowls and started putting the remnants of the steaks into the bowls for them. When he got to mine, and there was only the bone left, I smiled and waited for a comment.

There was a comment all right! He said, kind of seriously, "You were supposed to leave some for the dogs!" I lightheartedly laughed, noticing with everybody else's leftovers, there was more than enough for the dogs. But he was serious, and mumbled to himself that I should have known, and what's he going to do now? It got quiet. I had obviously broken the rules of the house.

Fortunately, someone broke the silence and said that it was time to call it a night. On the way home, we kept asking each other if he was serious, or why didn't he tell me before dinner? Or better yet, why didn't he cut some off for the dogs before serving his guests? The incident spoiled what would have otherwise been a perfect evening.

Our friend told us not to worry about it, but I knew we would never be invited back, and that was OK with us. It just goes to show you that interesting table tales aren't always in restaurants.

CHAPTER TWO

Cute Kids & Birthdays

CUTE KIDS

Sitting outside on the patio one afternoon, a little boy asked for a hamburger. His Dad said, "I'll have a hamburger, too, medium." Which prompted the young man to ask, "What other size do they come in?"

It was my friend's 8th birthday, and for his special celebration dinner, his parents told him that he could have anything that he wanted. Well, he wanted two orders of escargot. That was when they used to be served in their shells, with butter, garlic and parsley.

When I went to pick up the empty shells after he had utterly enjoyed them, the little boy said, "I've sucked 'em, but you can take them to the kitchen and finish sucking them if you want!"

It was a generous offer, but I graciously declined.

A little girl asked where her father was after he had gone to use the restroom. I told her that he had gone to see a man about a horse. When the Dad returned, the little girl called out, "Daddy, did you buy the horse?"

ME, TOO!

Birthdays come and go. There is nothing anyone can do about them. Everyone's in the same boat in this instance. One year something different arose. My birthday was approaching and I did not want it to be known, so I told my co-worker Alex that I would like to take next Wednesday off. He said, "Me, too." I was a little surprised, but continued that it was for a personal reason.

He again said, "Me, too." I looked a bit skeptical and finally told him it was for my birthday. He laughed and said, "Me, too! "

Then I really thought that he was just teasing me, and asked to see his drivers license. It was true. We have the same birthday. So instead of taking the day off, I made chocolate brownies, brought them to work, and we had a little party. I've worked with him for many years now, and we usually bring in a treat for ourselves that day, proudly announcing to anyone who will listen that it's *our* birthday.

A Special Birthday Surprise

When I was turning 50, I especially didn't want anyone to know, and went to work as usual. There was an unusual reservation on the book, Adnil for 4, at 6:00. I commented to my boss that the reservation looked suspicious to me. It looked like a trick my family might play on me. As kids, we spelled each other's names backwards and 'Adnil' was my nickname. My brother Mark, or 'Kram' and I still sometimes use those nicknames for each other. The boss assured me it was nothing of the sort, and told me to get my station ready for the night. I put the thought out of my head.

The restaurant was not that busy that night, and I had a table for four set by the window. At 6:00, I came out from the kitchen and noticed that there were two men at the table. They were dressed identically in green shirts, khaki slacks and sunglasses. Their elbows were on the table with the menus covering their faces. I mentioned that I knew they were waiting for two more, and that I would be back to discuss the specials for that evening. One of the men mumbled something inaudible, and I thought what strange people were sitting at that table.

Upon my returning to the table, two ladies had joined the men. I set down the glasses of water and bread while rattling off the specials when I noticed a strange quietness. I now looked down, and saw first one of my sisters, and then another one. I realized that the two identically-dressed men were my brothers-in-law. I was shocked, and surprised at myself that I had not known them right away. My sisters live about 3 hours away, and they were the last people that I normally expected to see at the restaurant. The men had come in first with the instruction to scope the situation with 'no significant eye contact' to alert me. As they were sitting by by the window, they then motioned to my sisters who were waiting in the car to come in after I had gone back to the kitchen.

My boss was in on the planning, and had helped to set up the surprise. When the realization hit me, he was standing behind me. He told me to take off my apron, sit down and enjoy dinner with my family. I immediately ordered a drink. My sisters had brought a cheesecake for dessert, and we had a wonderful meal. They brought a large gold cardboard sign that read 50, and I wanted the sign taken down, but the cat was already out of the bag, and everyone knew not only that it was my birthday, but how old I was...oh, well.

While we were having our little party, one of my regular customers joked that she would only eat if I got up from my table and waited on her. I told my sisters to grab napkins, fold them over their arms like waiters and go out to the customer to take her order, reminding them to mention the london broil special that night. My customer got a kick out of that.

I later mentioned to the boss that I had known something was up since Adnil just couldn't be anyone's real name! It was a lot of fun, a memorable birthday, and I'm grateful to my family for tricking me in such a fabulous way.

CUTE OLDER WOMAN

The reservation mentioned a birthday celebration. We were to prepare the table for a woman who was turning 91. In marched a perky lady smartly dressed in blue, with a matching woolen hat decorated by a long pheasant feather.

She was quite cute. When it came time for the birthday song, rather than cower like some people do, this 91-year-old stood up. She raised her arms as if to include the entire restaurant crowd, sang along, and then took a bow. Everyone dining at the restaurant that night enjoyed her vitality and exuberance.

LITTLE CAMPER

One evening I noticed an acrid smell upon entering the dining room. The source soon became apparent. A small boy was burning something over the decorative candle on the table. His parents noticed simultaneously, and reacted quickly to douse the fire. As the room filled with the smoke, the little boy was being scolded and protesting loudly, "But I was only roasting my french fry!"

HOW EMBARRASSING!

In a very elegant, refined dining room, a smartly dressed young boy ran out of the ladies room where his mother had taken him, and clearly stated out loud, "Daddy! Daddy! I didn't have to wash my hands! Mommy held it for me!"

ANOTHER SHARED BIRTHDAY

I share a birthday with one of my customers, so naturally feel an affinity towards him. Besides the dinners that I serve him throughout the year, he always comes into the restaurant on our birthday and we celebrate the day. I make sure he has a good table, bring him a favorite main course, and when the obligatory song is sung, I stand with him and include myself.

In the early years of our friendship, my birthday pal often brought dates to the restaurant. When he brought one special lady friend to meet me, asking my opinion, I felt honored. I approved of her and they married. I was even privy to personal conversations about whether or not to expand their family. It was not that unusual for me to hear such conversations, because couples discuss intimacies over dinner, but for them to include me was special. I considered us friends.

He and his wife always asked for me at the restaurant, and I made sure they were well taken care of. I even gave them a larger than usual dish of ice cream, which they dubbed a 'Linda scoop'. Apparently other waiters didn't have the same heavy hand with the ice cream scooper.

Their daughter is in her teens now. Life is busy and I don't see them as regularly as I used to. But the adage still applies: if you want extra ice cream in our restaurant, just come in and prove to me that we share a birthday.

CHAPTER THREE

Funny Jokes & Funny Food

JOKESTER WAITRESS

I started telling jokes publicly when I went away to college. When I was a kid, my Dad often brought home dirty jokes from work. Mom would say, "Don't tell the kids those jokes," but my brother and I absorbed them all. We still recount jokes to each other whenever we get together.

One thing about jokes is they have to be either appropriate or spontaneous. You have to be careful. You don't want to offend anybody, and if it's not timely, it's not funny. There is an art and talent to it, which some people just have and fortunately, God gave it to me. I have some appropriate jokes, like the chocolate ice cream (*see the No Chocolate story*), and the frogs legs (*see the Funny Food story*), but often people just say something and it reminds me of a joke.

As a waitress, I can get bored just repeating the specials and the regular chat, so I entertain myself as well as the customers by telling funny stories. I always laugh at these jokes, even though I've heard them or told them repeatedly *ad nauseum* as it may seem to the poor bartenders and my co-workers.

A co-worker came in one day and told me that he and his family had been to a party over the weekend and he found himself telling jokes, ones he had heard me repeat. He didn't realize that he knew them, but the jokes popped into his head, one after another. He entertained the party and was surprised at his repertoire. Now, when a customer asks for a joke, and I'm not sure, I ask that particular co-worker which one I should tell. He always comes up with a favorite.

There are times when customers demand a joke. They are used to hearing them and won't take no for an answer. Sometimes there are people at the table I don't know, and if I'm not their waitress, I have no feel for the table, so I can't just 'tell a joke'. I don't like to disappoint people but the joke telling has to come naturally, or it won't be funny. It helps when a customer tells a joke. That sort of reminds me of others, and also sets the tone for what is appropriate, and then the fun can begin. Sometimes to placate people, I rattle off something and, sure enough, it isn't appropriate or topical, and just doesn't work.

I tell jokes to priests, policemen, little old ladies, drunks and regulars who have heard them all and need to hear new material. All these audiences have to be taken into account, and I pick and choose which story I recount.

Once a couple asked the boss to insure that I never wait on them again. When the boss asked what had happened, they said, "She joked with us and she doesn't even know us!" The boss told me about the situation and asked me to be careful in the future. Time went on and I eventually became friends with the couple, but initially they were offended by my presumption.

Another time I was at the County Fair when one of my customers who had had too many beers, came up to me and demanded, "Joke me!" I was caught off guard, came out with something–of course not funny–and he went away a little disappointed. As I said, it has to be timely.

Over the years, my repertoire has grown and I now have a reputation as a joke teller as well as a waitress. I sometimes surprise people when I tell them my motto...dress like a nun, talk like a truck driver.

FUN WITH LUNCH

One day there was an important meeting at lunch with four at the table, my boss and three bankers. One of the bankers had been my customer for many years and I knew her quite well. I was extremely professional during the meal.

At the end of the meal, when it came time for the bill to be signed, I handed the folder to my boss. He signed it as usual, but added a hand written note. As he was handing it back to me, he casually asked if I could read it. He was being nice, and showing me that he had written in a nice tip for me.

I could see that their meeting was over and things had relaxed at the table, so I thought that a little levity was in order. Instead of thanking him for the tip, I read out loud, "Meet me in the parking lot in ten minutes." The boss and the whole table laughed. I told him afterwards that I tried to be good, but had to maintain my reputation for having some fun with lunch.

Joking Around with Money

Money is a serious subject, and I take it seriously because I am responsible for the accounting at the end of the day. This doesn't mean that I can't joke around when the bill comes.

Sometimes when customers run up a surprisingly large tab, to soften the shock, I tell them that the extra charges are for my trip to San Diego. I'm not sure why I use San Diego. I happened to say it one day, and the customers thought it was funny. Their responses are varied. If they say, "That's not enough to get there!" I tell them that I'm going to take the bus! If they say, "That's a lot of money just for San Diego!" I may give them a silly answer like, "Mother's getting older, and the sailors don't party for free anymore!"

Other times when I bring a rather large bill to a table, I will look into my pocket and pretend to count my tips. "Let me see if I can cover this tonight...no, not tonight."

When I'm not sure who in a large group will pay the bill, I try to find out in a humorous way. My favorite approach: "I figured out who the President is, and the Sergeant at Arms..." pointing to someone who seems to be a bit more vocal than the others. When the laughter dies down, I add, "But who is the Treasurer?"

WATCH OUT FOR THE ELEGANT ONES

Appearances can be deceiving. Highly esteemed socialites can sometimes let their hair down and surprise you. As an example of this, a very wealthy, well-dressed lady in this affluent county used to tell me jokes when she and her husband came into the restaurant. Some of them were downright raunchy, in fact, I would hesitate to repeat them.

They were funny to be sure, but something I would expect to hear in a bar filled with rough, hard-working men. So to hear them from this elegant woman made me raise my eyebrows, and taught me that you can't judge a book by its cover.

BEAUJOLAIS

"It's not the guys you date, it's the Beaujolais!" Say it out loud, and you will understand my joke that won me a bottle of wine.

One of my customers was a wine distributor who had ordered a bottle of Beaujolais, and was treated to my little joke. He chuckled and told me that in all his years in the business, he had never heard that one before, "It deserves a bottle of wine!"

He gave me his business card, and a few weeks later, I dropped by his store. He remembered me and gave me a nice bottle of Pinot Noir (not Beaujolais), plus some corkscrews which a waitress can always use.

I was happy that my little joke and sense of humor was appreciated. I had made a new friend and found a new place to shop for wines.

No Chocolate

One time, I swear, we were out of chocolate ice cream. I'm in the habit of listing our desserts and ice cream flavors: chocolate, vanilla, spumoni, mountain blackberry, etc. That day as I recited the selection to a family, I stopped myself and said "Excuse me, but we're out of chocolate." I continued on with my list, when the dad says, "I'll have the chocolate."

I answered, "I did mention chocolate, but we're out of it tonight." Dad thinks he's funny and repeats, "I'll have the chocolate." I said, "You know, there's a joke about that," and proceeded to tell the following story:

> A clerk in the ice cream store is waiting on a customer. The customer asks for a scoop of vanilla and a scoop of chocolate. The clerk tells him that they're out of chocolate. So the customer asks for a scoop of strawberry and a scoop of chocolate. The clerk reiterates, "I'm sorry, but we're out of chocolate." The customer apologizes and says that he's had a long day, and asks for a scoop of orange sherbet and a scoop of chocolate.
>
> Now the clerk gets mad and says, "Hey Buddy! Can you spell the van in vanilla?" The customer says: VAN. The clerk then asks, "Can you spell the straw in strawberry?" Why, yes, says the man: STRAW. Then the clerk asks him if he can spell the f*** in chocolate, and the customer responds, "There's no f*** in chocolate!" The clerk smiles, "That's what I'm trying to tell you!"

Everybody at the table laughed, and then their little boy quietly whispered to his brother, "I think the waitress just told Dad to f*** off!"

Funny Jokes Come with Funny Food

Restaurant employees all love food. It's the one thing we should have in common. When customers tell me that I seem excited to recite a special or describe a particular dish, I tell them that I love food, and get excited by it. I couldn't sell used cars!

At the Basque restaurant, my boss sits at the bar and sometimes eats unusual things. Basques say that they don't eat steak every day, "We kill an animal and eat it until it's gone." Hence, the sweetbreads, tripe and tongue on the menu. When customers come in and see the boss sitting at the bar, obviously enjoying his meal, they often say, "I'll have what he's having!" I'm not afraid to tell them, "No, you won't!" It might be pigs feet, or head cheese, or possibly Rocky Mountain Oysters. I learned to eat many things at the restaurant. One of my favorite unusual items is sea urchin. It's a formidable looking animal with a hard spiny shell. Inside is a bright orange flesh, delicious eaten raw, with chopped onions and hot sauce. One of the boss' brothers came from Santiago, Chile, and prepared it for us.

If my customer doesn't finish his salad, I often say, "Don't worry, in this restaurant, you don't have to eat the rabbit food, you can eat the rabbit!"

❧❧❧

We serve clams in their shells. One little girl wanted to keep all the shells to take to school for Show and Tell. Kids are enthralled with the escargot shells in the same way and sometimes ask to keep them. I put the clam shells in a little To Go bag for this cute little girl. I heard months later, after the family had moved to Florida, that the little girl had never thrown out the smelly shells. The family found them where she had packed them in her suitcase. All her clothes had to be thrown out.

We also have frog legs on the menu. They come frozen from several different places. The Chef prefers them fresh but told me that in the United States, the only place you can get commercial fresh frog legs is in Louisiana. That may have changed since Hurricane Katrina hit. We serve them with butter and garlic. I call them 'fish on a stick'.

One summer, we couldn't get any frog legs. I asked the distributor why and he told me they were held up at the docks. The frog legs were coming in from Indonesia, and DEA agents had found smuggled cocaine in with the packages. So all the frog legs were being kept and inspected. A few months later, all was cleared and our customers were once again able to order them.

The frog legs come paired up, shaped like little lady's legs. One time the prep cooks were thawing them out, and 'sat them' on the shelf, little legs just sitting there. Then the cooks arranged them in suggestive positions. We were hysterical with laughter! The Chef came in, and just said, "Don't play with the food."

When I think it is appropriate, and my customers order the frog legs, I often tell them my favorite frog jokes:
"What do you call a frog without legs? It doesn't matter, because it won't come anyway."
"What do you call a frog with legs? Dinner!"

Oh my goodness! A restaurant that serves frog and a waitress that tells frog jokes. We may be unique in this area.

ROCKY MOUNTAIN SPRINGTIME

Basques are famous as sheepherders. In the springtime, the sheep are gelded. In Basque tradition, the testicles are collected as a delicacy. They arrived in a big pot in the kitchen one day. I inquired what was in the big pot, and was told they were Rocky Mountain Oysters for the feast on Sunday.

Our neighbor, Eugenio, a Basque man from Spain, was in charge of the preparation. The testicles were marinated in red wine, garlic and spices for a few days. Eugenio checked on them, stirring them occasionally. Posters were put up in the restaurant announcing the annual event: All You Can Eat, Rocky Mountain Oysters Luncheon, with wine included, for $10 per person!

Sunday rolled around. We set out a long table with salad, bread, wine and of course the main course, sheep testicles. All the employees sat down, along with about 25 friends and neighbors to enjoy the seasonal specialty.

One elegant neighbor, Marie Claire, was not at all squeamish. She surprised me by saying, "You and me! Let's sit next to the balls!" We then sat down near the center of the table and the large bowl of delicacies was directly in front of us. I was at first apprehensive, but have to admit, they were absolutely delicious.

FUNNY AND STINKY

One of the boss' cousins came back from Spain with a gastronomical treat. It was some very stinky cheese that made Limburger seem sweet smelling. I actually like Limburger cheese, so could eat this stinky cheese. It tasted very good spread on crusty French bread.

Some of our favorite customers came in and the cousin wanted to be gracious and share his treat. The cheese was packed in water in a jar. As soon as the jar was cracked open in the dining room, an inexcusable odor escaped. An immediate uproar ensued. "UGH, what is that?" Some of us laughed, but a lot of people gagged. Needless to say, the guests did not partake, and the cheese jar was banished from the dining room.

A beautiful wheel of blue cheese was standing in the kitchen, waiting to be cut up in slices, and crumbled for salad dressing. I cut off a large hunk and put it in my mouth. Yum! When I was young, my mother often ate a piece of blue cheese just by itself and I couldn't imagine why. Time changes many things.

As I wandered around the restaurant with this lovely blue cheese slowly dissolving in my mouth, one of my co-workers standing behind me proclaimed loudly, "What is that funky smell?"

Slightly embarrassed, I turned around and admitted that it was me! With head hung low, I slowly went back to the kitchen, and afterwards knew that you couldn't just steal blue cheese without everyone knowing about it.

❧❧❧

One day, the boss' brother came in, as was his habit, and prepared a very large bowl of soup for himself. He had his own bowl and spoon, both oversized, as he was a large, hard-working man from the old country. He never married, probably because he had an old-fashioned view that would not seem attractive to modern women. He once told me that he needed to find a wife. This surprised me, as I considered him a confirmed bachelor. He said, "Yeah, I need someone to wash my socks." Who could resist such a romantic proposal!

So, on this particular day, the brother wandered into the dining room with his oversize bowl of soup and a horrendous smell filled the room. All the employees were running around trying to figure out what could be causing this bad odor, as it wafted about us, but we couldn't identify it.

When the boss' brother was leaving, I happened to ask him what he had been doing all day. He responded, "I've been spreading manure!" Apparently, he was right. He did need someone to wash his socks!

CHAPTER FOUR

Developing My Skills

Ice Cream Fountain

Early in my career, I was working at a nationally known chain famous for many flavors of ice cream. I suddenly had easy access to delicious food and desserts and really packed on the pounds that summer treating myself to a slice of coconut cake with coconut ice cream nearly every night.

I worked hard to learn everything, even when the boss decided that we should be selling cocktails. I was still in high school and underage to be drinking or serving. The boss didn't want to pay a bartender, so he told us to read the bartender's manual and make drinks. All my high school friends came in and ordered drinks so I could practice my new skills. For some reason, scotch sours were popular. I was making them from scratch with sugar and lemon, and they were easy for teenagers to drink. All of this underage stuff was very illegal.

My most memorable order was for a Grasshopper. I didn't know that one, so I looked it up in the manual. The ingredients started with Crème de Menthe: I grabbed some of that and put it in the blender. Crème de Cocoa came next. In it went. Then the recipe called for cream. Well, our restaurant specialized in ice cream, so they wanted us to use vanilla ice cream instead of cream. I put in a scoop of vanilla, and whirred away. The frothy drink looked good and inviting except for the all-white appearance and a lone blueberry floating in circles. At the time I did not realize there were two kinds of Crème de Menthe: one was green, obviously, for 'Grasshopper' and the other one clear. I had grabbed the clear one. As for the blueberry, the blueberry ice cream container was right next to the vanilla and apparently we had a bit of contamination.

My customer at first was taken aback, but upon tasting the new creation, pronounced it, "Fabulous!" From then on, his Grasshopper was always white, foamy and minty with a garnish of blueberry, my contribution to mixology.

That summer I worked my way up to the front station where I was busier and made more money. One night there was a table of four, who left me a $5 tip, much more than the few quarters I was accustomed to. By the end of the evening, I remember that I made $30. It was such a large amount of money at the time that I woke my mother up when I got home and told her. She said, "That's nice, dear" and went back to sleep. Just to show you how significant that amount was, four years later when I was in college, I rented a room for $50 a month. The excitement of that night made me want to be a waitress for the rest of my life.

COCKTAIL EXPERIENCE REQUIRED

The newspaper listing in the Help Wanted section caught my attention, and I thought, That's for me! After all, I was now a seasoned bartender, with my previous experience at the ice cream fountain. I thought I could handle anything, even as a cocktail server in a nightclub, now that I was old enough.

I put on my best dress, some open shoes and applied. It turned out to be a job in a disco, with late hours, unsavory characters and a shady nightclub owner. I was insulted to be offered the position of Coat Check Girl but decided to try it anyway.

After a few hours I asked to leave, saying that the environment was not for me. The owner looked me up and down and asked if I was sure. Nodding, I turned to leave and heard him say, "I was going to make you mine!"

I needed a job at the time, but all I could envision was this man as a pimp, in a flashy car with ladies hanging on his arm. I got out of there as quickly as possible, and thought twice about my confidence with cocktails. Early morning coffee shops were sure to be better than this!

THE PALACE HOTEL

One of my early jobs was at the Palace Hotel in San Francisco. The city has a history of the grand hotels as meeting places with the Palace being one of the most notable. Opening in 1875, it cost $5 million to build, an incredible sum for the time, demonstrating the vast wealth from the Gold Rush. Opulent furnishings were brought around the Horn from the East Coast by clipper ships. The original builder, William Chapman Ralston, never got to see it open. He was found dead in San Francisco Bay prior to the grand opening, and it was never discovered if it was foul play or suicide due to the immense debt he incurred from the building of the hotel.

A wonderful book entitled *Bonanza Inn,* written by Oscar Lewis and Carroll D. Hall, details the construction, the furnishings, the specific silverware ordered, and the employees that comprised this monumental Palace. When I worked there, there was still an old tunnel in the basement that went underground to the bank across the street to prevent any problems with the transfer of the day's receipts.

I was first hired in the coffee shop that opened at 6 AM. My shift was Thursday through Sunday, 5 AM to 1 PM. I rode the bus into San Francisco early in the morning along with financial district workers, stock brokers and secretaries. As we drove over the Golden Gate Bridge, I could see the fishing boats going out to sea at 4:30 AM with their tiny lights way below the bridge. When I walked to work from the bus, San Francisco was just waking up. Shop owners would be hosing down the sidewalks in front of their establishments, preparing for the day.

I was usually good at getting up on Thursday, Friday, and even Saturday, but by the time Sunday came around, the hotel often had to call me, as I was still in bed. The manager asked if I would like a later shift. My answer was, "Yes, please!" He moved me into the fancy dining room to serve lunch. That shift didn't start until 10:30 AM, and I could ride the ferry in, a beautiful way to commute on San Francisco Bay. There was a bar open on the ferry. Coffee, tea and yes, Bloody Marys! I was surprised by the amount of booze being served at 10:00 in the morning. The ferry ride home at 4:30 PM turned into a rousing party. I think the Golden Gate Transit Service made a lot of money on the refreshments.

Working my way up from a coffee shop waitress to a dining room server took a little adjustment by the all-male staff. In the past, women servers in the dining room had been unreliable, routinely absent due to monthly female matters. My male co-workers were surprised when I kept showing up regularly and they ultimately accepted me.

I actually didn't open a bottle of wine at the table by myself for many months, because the older waiters did it for me. "Oh no, Linda, let me do the presenting!" The  protocol was very important to them. I finally put my foot down and assured the professional waiters that I was up to the important task of properly serving wine.

I was at the Palace Hotel through a lot of difficult, as well as interesting times. One of the unforgettable weekends involved a Science Fiction convention held at the hotel. Costumed aliens were roaming the halls, and many of the attendees didn't believe in booking a room. The hotel security staff kept finding them camped in the hallways.

Another memory is of the annual San Francisco Cotillion held in the gorgeous Garden Court dining room, where the young girls were elegantly dressed and presented to Society. I observed many of these formal functions standing on the sidelines, watching from the doorway of the restaurant.

I was at work at the Palace in San Francisco the day Mayor George Moscone and Harvey Milk were shot by Supervisor Dan White. White ultimately used the now infamous 'Twinkie Defense,' saying that he had had too much sugar that day. It was a painful day, and one I'll never forget.

The Palace was unionized and one year there was a strike. The strike put an end to my commuting and my days at the Palace Hotel. It was a month long, and during that time, I found other work. But the Palace will always remain a special part of my time in San Francisco.

THE OLD PALACE WAITER

One of the memorable waiters I worked with at the Palace was in his seventies. He had worked at the hotel for 50 years. He showed us pictures of himself as a young pugilist, in a pose with boxing shorts and gloves taken sometime in the twenties. He seemed to do very well for himself, having a good position in the hotel, and he knew everybody.

The waiter was charming and well known by the customers. When 11:30 AM rolled around and it was time to open for lunch, the other waiters and I would all hang out in the kitchen drinking coffee, except the old waiter. He was at the door greeting everyone that walked by on Market Street, shaking hands and guiding them to his station. When his station was full, the rest of us could all then go to work, taking the overflow.

The old waiter lived in an apartment on Hyde Street, and I learned that he owned the whole building. I asked him once how he accomplished that on a waiter's salary. He said that in the old days, he worked lunch, dinner and then room service between meals which meant that he worked almost 13 hours a day.

He also told me that he made most of his money before the days of the duplicate check system. He reminded me that the system provides a carbon copy to the kitchen of what is ordered and the duplicate goes to the cashier, thereby insuring that items are correctly accounted.

This man calmly explained to me that in the old days, he'd take the order from the customer, write the order check and give it to the kitchen. Then at the end of the meal, he would collect from the customer and go to the cashier to pay for the table. Some customers ordered chicken dinners and some had tea and toast. The waiter rewrote the checks and pretended that most of his tables had only the tea and toast. Oh, I thought to myself, you pocketed the difference!

I worked with this interesting gentleman for three years and was invited to his home for wonderful Greek dinners. He was a classic, colorful San Francisco character, one of many, that helped me understand what makes San Francisco special.

DEBONAIR DISHWASHER

When I was commuting to San Francisco, I waited at my local bus stop every morning. On Mondays, I noticed a little debonair man waiting for the bus with me. He was always sharply dressed, carrying a leather valise.

One Monday he said to me, "Young Lady, I work right here and see you every day. Where do you go?" I told him that I worked as a waitress at one of the larger hotels in the city. He said, "Why don't you work here?" pointing to the small family-owned restaurant, The Chalet Basque. He was their dishwasher and lived on the premises except on Mondays, his day off. That's when he went into San Francisco to his little apartment.

A short time later, I needed a new job and went to the Basque. I told the owner that Georges, the dishwasher, whom I had met on the bus, recommended me. As it turned out, I had met the Patron before when he had admired our car, a Citroen, and he remembered me. He said, "You with the French car, you can start Tuesday," the famous line that turned my job into a career.

I worked with Georges for eight years. He wore a leather apron and worked day and night, except on his day off. When the evening was drawing to a close, he'd swing open the kitchen doors, and yell, "Any more monkeys?" He was asking if there were any more customers, and did he have any more dishes or glasses from the tables that needed to be washed. From then on, I referred to the customers as monkeys. "Table 3, how many monkeys?" And I extended the analogy by calling money 'bananas.' So, the monkeys paid with bananas, 34 bananas, 100 bananas, when I counted out the change, all because of Georges.

Georges had owned mules when he lived in France, and had a rapport with them. He told me once about accepting a wager from a priest. The bet was to back Georges' mules out of the barn, strapped to a cart. The mules accomplished the feat and Georges won the bet. He explained that the mules listened to him because he fed them sugar cubes with rum.

Short, stocky, and rotund, Georges was very strong and determined. Once crossing an empty parking lot, carrying a case of wine, he ran right into the Chef. Georges didn't move left or right, he just came straight through regardless of what or who was in his way. He carried racks of hot glasses, straight from the dishwasher and right over the customers' heads, often dripping on them. Sometimes it was funny and sometimes it wasn't.

Once Georges was in the dining room relaxing, sitting on a chair, showing his big belly. His legs were out to either side, and his elbow rested on the table, as he smoked a cigarette. A small boy went up to him and asked, "Are you a fat man?" Georges took a long draw on his cigarette and said proudly, "Yes, I am."

Several years later, when it was time to retire, Georges decided to go back to France. He cleaned out his room at the restaurant and gave me his armoire, not a fancy one, but I cherish it. It was a difficult decision, he said, to return to France. The 'assurance' (French health insurance) was better, but there was no late night TV!

I kept in contact with him through postcards and he always addressed me as *Fillette*, the young lady he met on the bus.

HONESTY PAYS!

While working a lunch shift, my sharp eyes spied a roll of money under a table. The customers had just left. I did not know who they were but they had been conversing with a neighboring table. I then asked the other table if they knew who had been sitting next to them, and was told that it was their friend, the banker. I telephoned the bank and discreetly asked to speak to the man, and mentioned that he had left something behind at the restaurant. He returned right away. Apparently, he realized that he had misplaced four hundred dollars in cash that was supposed to have been deposited before he went to lunch. It belonged to a customer of his, so he was very appreciative when I returned it to him.

The next day, the banker walked into the restaurant early, before we had opened. All the employees were seated around a table enjoying lunch before the rush of the day. He came right over to me and handed me forty dollars, and an exquisite bottle of white Bordeaux from his extensive wine collection.

The extra reward was that he did this in front of all my co-workers, and my boss. One of my co-workers yelled out rather indiscreetly, "Did you see that? She got forty dollars!"

I recently saw the banker and his wife and even though it has been many years, we both remember the incident. It helped me to establish my reputation for honesty, which is something money can't buy.

CHAPTER FIVE

A Certain Basque Flavor

THE CHALET BASQUE

I first met Raymond, the original owner of the Chalet Basque, when he introduced himself as we stood in front of our French car, a Citroen Deux Chevaux. It had Parisian license plates, was very cute and often got us a lot of attention. He casually mentioned that if I ever needed a job, to come see him. Later on, when I was looking for a new job, I applied at The Basque. He remembered me and made the now famous comment, "You with the French car, you can start Tuesday."

I was one of the few non-European employees at the Chalet Basque, and felt honored to be included. I had spent time in Europe, including three visits to France. My knowledge of the French language was basic, but has improved over the years.

Working for Raymond, I came to see what a remarkable man he was. He was a fair man who worked hard and expected everyone to do the same. He befriended many over the years. I tried to count how many couples and families he helped, sponsoring them to come to the United States or just people like me who ended up making a comfortable living at his establishment. I lost count.

Recently, his wife Jeannie told me, "Thirty-seven years ago on this day, Raymond and I drove past this property and decided to buy it and open up a Basque restaurant"...bringing one of Raymond's dreams to fruition. They were both from France, but had met in San Francisco where Raymond had been working as a gardener. There was a plaque hanging in the restaurant that read, *Gardeners don't get old, they just lose their bloomers.*

The building had been a local hamburger joint. Some of the neighbors were slow to accept the transformation into a nice restaurant. My uncle, who lived close by, warned me away from there, saying it had a bad reputation with a lot of motorcycles. True, it is on a road out to China Camp State Park, and motorcyclists and bicyclists often go riding out past the restaurant, but as for the big, bad motorcycle parties...well, let's just say, I've been waiting!

But Raymond and Jeannie persevered. Luckily, one mile away was the newly built Marin County Civic Center designed by Frank Lloyd Wright. The Civic Center crowd helped to establish the restaurant, but it was Raymond and his wife's personality that kept it going.

In the beginning, it was slow. There was a big corporation in the area. Raymond noticed that the office workers weren't coming to lunch very often. So he drove over to the corporate office and asked why. The execs told Raymond it was because the employees drank too much when they went there. Raymond offered to solve the problem by bringing lunch to them. They accepted gratefully. Raymond packed up maybe 10 or 12 lunches a day and drove them over. It started his reputation as a purveyor of fine food, and as an astute businessman.

It is interesting to note, that the original menu offered Boeuf Bourguignon or Coq au Vin, complete dinner for $3.75, with children's dinner half price! Two questions come to mind: what is half of $3.75, and did anyone notice that the same wine sauce was used for both dishes? Now, that's economy!

Ultimately the neighbors got to know Raymond and liked having a friendly watering hole nearby, and the business thrived. It was the kind of place where a woman could stop by for a drink, see friends and be comfortable. One night I found myself locked out of the house. This was before cell phones, and my only alternatives were to wait on our cold front porch until my man came home, or go down the street and wait in the well-lit restaurant. That was the first time I went into the Chalet Basque and was warmly received by Raymond.

After I started working at the Chalet Basque, my commute was walking down the street. I no longer took the bus with Georges, the Debonair Dishwasher. Now I was working with him.

I tell my customers that even though I lived down the street from The Basque, we didn't go to dinner there too often. It being so close, I felt that we hadn't 'been out' unless we'd gone for a drive. When the neighbors from the house behind the restaurant come to dinner, I try to seat them in the front dining room, so they don't have to see their back yard, and therefore feel they're 'out'.

Another neighbor, as a favor, filled in as a waitress for a few weeks with us, and she told everybody to be careful, "If you eat here often enough, you'll end up working here!"

It's hard to describe the feeling of being at one establishment so long that you feel you belong. I walked up the street regularly for so many years that one real estate broker told a prospective buyer she didn't need a clock, "Linda will walk by everyday precisely at 5:00!" Even after I moved to another town, I still came to work at 'my neighborhood place'. I like my new town and although there are many good places to eat and for me to work, there is no place that feels like home as much as the Basque.

GO ACROSS THE STREET

Raymond was a good boss. He supported his waitresses all the way. If he had a problem with something I did, he quietly mentioned it in the privacy of the kitchen. He was a no-nonsense man and did not accept 'monkey business', as he called it.

One afternoon at the Chalet Basque, Raymond asked a large party to leave. There were fourteen in the party, sitting at a long table. When they first arrived, they said they had never been there before. They were hesitant about sitting at the table we had set for them, not sure if it was to their liking. They complained about the people smoking in the enclosed, designated smoking area. Then they sent back the wine that they had just ordered and I had opened for them. They said there was nothing the matter with the wine, they had just changed their mind. The wine happened to be a very good one, the favorite of the boss' wife, Jeannie!

I had to tell Raymond about the wine because I had to return the bottle to the bar and explain what had happened. He had heard all the complaints from that party, and had let things slide, but when the perfectly good wine came back, it was just too much.

He went out to the table, calmly picked up the menus, and started clearing their table, telling them, "Go across the street." This was particularly funny, since we were in a rural area, and there were only hills and trees 'across the street' from us.

The whole party got up and left through the back door, never to be seen again.

PARTY TIMES AT THE BASQUE

The turnover at the Chalet Basque was minimal. Only once in a while did we have new people to work with. Our core group of employees spent a lot of time together at work and also after hours. I once mentioned to a co-worker that we seemed to be spending more time with each other than with our families.

Some of our memorable occasions were when we all went out to be served by others. One Christmas, the owner said he wanted to do something different. Rather than have the party at our place, we all went out to a neighboring restaurant. It was a fine time, but they made a mistake with the order and the Chef's dinner got delayed! He made light of it, pretended to eat the azalea which adorned the table and commented on how they thought he was too fat to eat. He was a nice man, not too fat really, but said, "Next year, we'll stay at our restaurant, where I know I'll get fed!"

After that we always had our holiday parties at our restaurant, either on Monday, the day we were closed or sometimes on Saturday during the afternoon, when we all had to work that night. On one such occasion, the party was set for noon on Saturday. We had a gorgeous seven-course Christmas meal with cocktails, and wine. There was a boombox, so we had music and such as you may call it, dancing. We had a grand time and the afternoon rolled on. Soon it was time to open the restaurant and we all went to work. One of the customers complained to the boss, "Your whole crew is drunk!" The boss said, rather matter of factly, "Yes, I know," then wished him a Merry Christmas.

When we had these parties, the food was always exceptional. There was an appetizer, our famous home-made liver pate, with salami and hot peppers. Then soup was served, usually a light consomme. The Chef said the soup should be light when you're having a large meal. The fish course was next. It consisted of salmon, with a cream tarragon sauce, or maybe prawns with garlic. For the main entree, either a small Rack of Lamb, perhaps a sirloin, thinly sliced like London Broil, or a petite Filet Mignon with a mushroom Madeira sauce. Yum! Salad came after, served with a cheese plate, sheepherders cheese and some Roquefort.

And of course, we didn't forget the dessert! Cherries Jubilee was a favorite, or a marzipan-covered Princess cake, or something homemade that I brought in. I consider myself a baker and often bring cakes to these events. Sometimes I apologize because the cake has not turned out as I had hoped,

but the Chef's wife always told me, "Bring it anyway, and we'll let you know if it's all right!"

I had a habit of sitting in a certain corner during these feasts, next to one waitress. After a few years, she figured it out. "You sit in the corner so it's not easy for you to get up and help with the clearing." Since we all worked there, we were expected to help. Then she added, "And you sit next to me because you know I don't eat dessert and you can have mine!" I have to admit I was guilty as charged.

YOUNG FRENCH GIRL

My customers were from France and the parents did not speak a lot of English. However, the young daughter was quite confident of her language abilities. She proudly told me, "This is the only restaurant that we go to, except sometimes when we go out for burger cheese."

THE BEVADOR

"Come to see the Bevador!" read an advertisement for the restaurant. The Bevador is a tall bottle-shaped refrigerator that stands prominently in the corner of the bar area. This amazing refrigerator was already there when the restaurant was first purchased in 1961. It was then a Battleship Gray metal cylinder with a tapered top and even a pinched cap to finish off the look. It stands an impressive seven feet tall with a large brass latch and handle. The top lifts off to reveal the motor, so it is eminently repairable. It is showing its age, but still hums and often rattles.

In the '80s, Raymond found another Bevador, and brought it into the dining room. I was there the day of installation. These fabulous refrigerators each weigh about 800 pounds, and it took

Raymond, his son John, and Raymond's brother Sauveur a few hours to dolly it in the door, across the floor (watch the chandeliers!), and get it onto its platform. Jeannie and I sat at one of the tables, drinking red wine, and offering helpful comments to the three men as they labored. It was quite an event. After installation, it needed some new freon gas, but since then it has been very dependable, keeping the wine, beer and milk quite cold.

About that time, a friend and talented painter, Ken Kirkland, painted the Bevadors a light brown with dark brown accents and made them look like wood. They had always been impressive, but now they were gorgeous!

The Bevadors were built for the Golden Gate International Exposition in 1939, held on Treasure Island in the middle of San Francisco Bay. There were only 11 Bevadors produced, and we have two! A brass plaque on them reads:

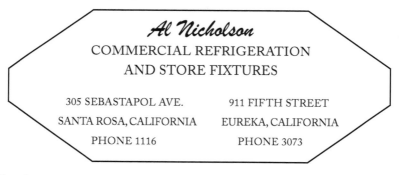

Al Nicholson
COMMERCIAL REFRIGERATION
AND STORE FIXTURES

305 SEBASTAPOL AVE.   911 FIFTH STREET
SANTA ROSA, CALIFORNIA   EUREKA, CALIFORNIA
PHONE 1116   PHONE 3073

They're still quite a conversation piece today. Customers always want to open the door and spin the revolving Lazy Susan shelves around, and perhaps help themselves to a beer.

LEFT OVER WINE

Sometimes people working in restaurants drink. It's part of the trade. I worked with one waitress who always had a glass of wine ready. There would be one on the shelf in the kitchen, one on the buffet in the dining room, and usually another one in the Bevador refrigerator.

The refrigerator has revolving shelves like a Lazy Susan. One day I opened the refrigerator, spun the shelf around to get something, and a half-full glass of wine tipped over and made a mess that I had to clean up.

When the waitress who was the usual suspect came in, I told her that she had left a glass of wine in the refrigerator, that it had spilled and I had to clean it up.

She replied, "You know it couldn't be me, I would never leave a glass half-full!"

PASSING ON THE LEGACY

When Raymond and Jeannie decided to retire after 25 years, they sold the restaurant to a former employee, a Basque named Francisco and his wife Antoinette. He had come to the United States from Spain years before, and had been employed by Raymond. Francisco was a hard worker and technically a waiter at the restaurant, but I often saw him up on the roof on his day off repairing, cleaning, doing anything that needed to be done.

Antoinette met Francisco when she filled in at the Chalet Basque for Raymond and Jeannie when they went to France. She had previously owned a French restaurant in San Francisco, and was the perfect person to watch the business while Raymond and Jeannie took a well-deserved vacation. I asked her a few years later what she remembered about working at the Basque all those years ago, and she replied, "I only remember Francisco," the man she married. As owners, Antoinette waited tables and was in charge of the business end, and Francisco was the front man, full of personality.

When they decided to retire, the restaurant was sold to yet another former employee. Back in 1970, Roger was invited by Raymond to be the Executive Chef. He had been at the top of his class in Paris. Roger envisioned a grand American venue, but it was a small, family-owned place in a quiet part of Marin County, north of San Francisco—not what he expected!

Roger shared a bedroom with the owner's son. He tells a story about how he got his privacy. Raymond apparently had found 'a good buy' and came home with many cases of wine, which ended up being stored in and thus dividing the bedroom. Any privacy is better than none!

After working at the restaurant for a few years, Roger moved on to open his own place. He had a few cafes with partners at first, but ultimately opened a very successful Basque restaurant in Sausalito called Guernica, which he ran for 27 years.

When Francisco and Antoinette decided to sell, I called Roger and said, "You have to buy the restaurant. It's for sale, and they're going to tear it down and build condominiums. You're the only one who can save it. I'll work for you." After much negotiating, Roger signed the papers a year later, and I've been working with him ever since and hopefully will continue when his son takes over.

Each boss had their own personality and following, but they were all restaurateurs in the sense of hospitality being a priority: old world charm, yet still keeping a look out for the business. Our customers are what keeps them and all of us going.

REMEMBERING RAYMOND

Earlier this year, Raymond passed away. I worked for him for 6 years, not as long as some, more than others, but this man had a profound effect on me. His passing was a great shock. We all miss him. I was honored by Jeannie and John when they asked me to speak at the church. This is the eulogy that I gave:

"It was a rainy day in San Rafael when Raymond Coscarat first introduced himself to Thor and me and wanted to know who owned the Citroen with Parisian plates. He was known about town for stopping in shops and restaurants getting to know the folks. As it happened, we lived down the street from his restaurant. He told me that if I ever needed a job, to come talk to him, and fatefully, a few years later, I did just that. He remembered our French car, and hired me on the spot. He added that he intended for me to stay. He didn't have a large turnover, and I guess I took that to heart. I'm still here 28 years later.

I wasn't the only one. Many here in this room, who spent years in Raymond and Jeannie's employ understand when I say we became a little family with connections that wove in and out of many lives—connections that endure. A lot of people speak of community, but Raymond and Jeannie built one. With son John at their side, with perseverance and hard work...against adversity and high water, they built the Chalet Basque, now an established landmark for neighbors and travelers alike to congregate, share a meal and feel at home.

Raymond invited me to be a part of that and I am grateful. He opened his heart and arms to us through friendship, employment and advice and always saw possibilities, helping others fulfill their dreams.

Raymond and Jeannie's Legacy: The Chalet Basque, where we've celebrated christenings, birthdays, weddings, and yes, funerals. We are here today celebrating Raymond's accomplishments and his enthusiasm for the wonder that is life."

After the church service, we all naturally went to the Chalet Basque. A grand luncheon was laid out for about 100 people. We all knew that none of this would have been possible without the dreams and foresight of Raymond.

Kitchen Quip

A man came in for dinner who was so fat, he needed room for two to sit comfortably. We don't mind. We're not here to judge. Besides, the restaurant likes it when people come in to eat a lot of food, which he clearly had. He was pleasantly surprised at the courses offered. We were serving family style: hors d'oeuvres, soup, salad and dessert all included with a hearty main course.

The fat man happily cleaned all his plates. He appeared to be completely satisfied with his meal. After laying his napkin down, he heaved an audible sigh of satisfaction, paid his bill and pushed himself up from the table. Rather than leave right away, he came towards the kitchen, swung the door open, and announced, "This is my kind of place!"

CHAPTER SIX

Memorable & Venerable

OLD CHARLEY

Old Charley wasn't always old. At one time he was a young American GI just home from WWII with an Austrian wife. He started pumping gas at our local gas station, and eventually worked at the station for fifty years. The son of the station owner told me that Charley was his Dad's best employee even considering himself. Charley knew all the neighbors, knew their cars, knew their families, knew their habits.

This young old man was Portuguese and loved to fish. He and his wife spent time fishing on San Francisco Bay for recreation, as well as commercially. For some reason, a lot of Portuguese who love to fish, can't swim, and that was Charley. "Never learned how," he told me.

Charley liked to drink, but his wife didn't approve, so it wasn't until after she died that we really got to know him. He was lonely, so he spent more afternoons with us at the bar. He told us how he missed her, always adding that she was a saint. He was comfortable because he had some money saved and owned his own home.

Then he met her, the Black Widow. They lived close by, and had known each other somewhat when their respective mates were alive, but didn't spend much time together. Time passed, they started seeing each other and commiserating about their shared experiences. Things were progressing. They became drinking buddies.

At one point the Black Widow decided that the young lady bartender had eyes for her Charley. Never mind the 35 plus years difference in age. Never mind the fact that the lady bartender was in love and engaged, and never mind that it just wasn't true! The Black Widow was the jealous type, and it caused a lot of discomfort. She was bad news, and all of us in the restaurant tried to warn Charley. We all told him, each in our turn, "Don't marry her! Don't marry her!" But he told us that they had a great physical relationship, which none of us wanted to envision. He sold his house, moved in and married her.

They traveled, drank and gambled until his money was gone. It took about five years. Then the Black Widow called Charley a drunk, kicked him out of the house, and to add insult to injury, got a restraining order against him.

At first, he was sort of homeless, staying with friends. Then he moved into a small trailer walking distance from the restaurant, and took up residence, literally, at one of the tables on the patio. It became known as Charley's table. He knew lots of people and became sort of an impromptu greeter, showing potential customers the restaurant's banquet rooms and reciting the hours of operation.

We all worried about him and different friends offered him rooms to rent, places to stay. He refused. I asked him why he didn't accept some of the offers for a nice house to live in. He said he wanted to stay near and watch the Black Widow's comings and goings. The Black Widow went to work, the Black Widow came home: every trip noted by Charley.

He ordered drinks but would never drink them all. People thought he drank all day, but he told me he only liked the first couple of sips. The teenagers in the neighborhood picked right up on this, and I noticed they were hanging around Charley— to finish his drinks. We put a stop to that!

We celebrated his birthdays and Christmases. The boss gave him a bill each month, probably for half of what he actually spent. Then Charley's landlord sold the property and he had to move from his trailer. He again refused offers from nice people willing to rent him a room. He refused the VA when they wanted him to stay at the Veteran's Home in Yountville.

In other words, he had options but none satisfactory to him.

Then, without talking to the boss, Charley moved into the laundry room at the restaurant He brought his sleeping bag, and told us that he'd be fine. This, obviously, would not do. The boss didn't want to kick him out, so he stayed in the laundry room for a few nights.

God intervened. Out of the blue, a younger brother of Charley's showed up in town for a high school reunion. When told of his brother's predicament, he came right away. Gathering up Old Charley, he took him back home with him to Idaho.

A month later, we got a letter with a forwarding address for Charley's mail. His brother said that Charley was settling in and spending time fishing. Customers still ask, "Where's Charley?" We tell them he's come full circle...he's gone fishing.

The Black Widow came into the restaurant a little while later and wanted to know Old Charley's whereabouts. She said, "It's the strangest thing! It's like he just disappeared!" None of us seemed to know where he was, and apparently none of his other friends would tell her either.

YOU REMIND ME...

I was stopped abruptly at the bar one night by a man who said I reminded him of his third wife. I said, "Really?" He replied, "Yes, your hair, how you walk and talk..." I was intrigued. Someone who looked like me? I paused for a moment. I wanted to hear more when he finished with the statement, "... and I've only been married twice!"

I've heard many a come-on line, but I thought that one was particularly clever and worth repeating.

MY FRIEND ESTHER

One of my favorite customers, Esther Faulk, passed away last year two months shy of her 104th birthday. I had met her about eight years before, when she came for lunch with her granddaughter Laura. On occasion, Esther's daughter Ruth and her great granddaughter Brook would also join us, having four generations at the table for lunch.

Esther was a charmer, and told us of her childhood in Pennsylvania, eating apples and learning how to roll cigars as her first job. The leaves of the tobacco had to be rolled gently, she said, and Esther was good at it. She mentioned that her older sister, Tilly, didn't get the job of rolling as often as she.

When Esther's sister Tilly turned 100, and was planning a big party in Seattle, Esther told me that she did not want to go. I asked her if the trip was too much for her. "No," she said, "... my sister always bosses me!" But Esther was just kidding, and did go. Tilly had a grand birthday celebration complete with a limousine. I saw photos of this most memorable party with all her family and friends.

One Christmas, Esther and her family gave me a pin of a miniature tea set in a beautiful gift box. People often asked about my unusual collar pin and I proudly told them it was a gift from my friend Esther! I wore that pin on my apron uniform until the clasp finally broke. But I still have it, to remind me of my dear friend.

Esther was married to her 'sweet sixteen', the love of her life. He was a guard at Alcatraz, the notorious island prison in the middle of San Francisco Bay. Hers was the first family to move onto the island after it became part of the Corrections Department. She lived on the island for 35 years, and in the mornings, put her children on the boat for San Francisco to go to school.

Esther liked to attend the annual reunions of the guard families after the closing of Alcatraz as a prison. She was well loved, and served as a center of support for the friends she made while living on the isolated island. She always told me about the upcoming reunions and how much she looked forward to seeing her old friends.

At the restaurant, Esther liked to pull out a picture of her long-deceased husband in his guard uniform, and gently caress it as if to smooth his hair and straighten his clothes. Then she would smile, reminding me that this was the love of her life.

One afternoon she was dining and in rolled a gentleman in a wheelchair. He was Judge William Angell, at the time aged 91 years, dapper as usual, holding court with his friends and telling resplendent stories of his life abroad in Paris, and of his years as District Attorney in Chicago.

I wanted him to meet Esther. You see, as DA of Chicago, Judge Angell had sentenced Al Capone to Alcatraz, and Esther's husband had been on deck to receive him when he arrived. Now there was a bit of history that the two could share, and I thought they might enjoy each other's company for lunch. I admit that I was playing matchmaker. When I introduced them, Judge Angell, a consummate gentleman and poet, promptly entertained Esther with a poem, "A star fell from the sky and lost its place, and now I see it shining in lovely Esther's face!"

Oh, how she melted! It was a pleasure to see her face light up. Nothing ever did come of the two of them, but I often marvel of the historical significance of those two, at the same place, years later with that Al Capone connection.

OLDER SMOKERS

My friend Greta was Danish, and known for smoking cigars. When Greta came to the restaurant, after dinner she sat outside on the patio to enjoy her smoke. She made the newspapers when her friend, Mr. Christian Mortensen, had a birthday and turned 114. The article mentioned that they often spent Mondays together, smoking cigars.

The journalist who wrote the newspaper article asked Mr. Mortensen the secret to his longevity. One of the reasons given was the well water he drank when he was a boy in Denmark. Mr. Mortensen also said he liked his vegetables. When asked what his favorite vegetable was, he said *frikadeller.* To translate, *frikadeller* are Danish meatballs. The journalist and his editor let this pass without checking, which gave the local Danish community a good laugh.

Greta called me one day to make arrangements for a party at the Chalet Basque. I asked her what the celebration was for, and she only answered that it was *her* party. The afternoon of the event, we received a very sad call. While getting ready for her 88th birthday party at the Basque, Greta collapsed in her apartment, lost consciousness and passed away. She had always been very spry and healthy. I believe it was the fall, and not the cigars that led to her demise.

Another lady smoker of note was Doris. Rather than cigars, she enjoyed pipes. Always very pretty, small, cute pipes, many different ones: some with metal inlays and others inset with semiprecious stones. She too would enjoy the solitude of the quiet smoke on the patio after dinner.

Our customers were never bothered by these lady smokers. They were intrigued by the fact that these were not young ladies, and the smoking invoked a certain level of class and sophistication.

The Adventures of Don and Vera

Meet Don and Vera Muggeridge, a British couple I met at the restaurant. I have spent many an evening getting to know them and listening to their exciting adventures. World War II played a large part in their experiences, as it did for everyone else at the time. They had vivid memories of the events, 70 years later.

Don volunteered for the Royal Corps of Signals in 1939 and saw service in France with the British Expeditionary Force. He told me that he had been there for two or three days when on May 8, 1940, "All hell broke loose!" The Germans came, as he tells it 'armoured as well as Luftwaffe', on land and in the air, wave after wave, and sent Don and all the Allied forces into retreat back to the beaches of Dunkirk. It was a harrowing experience that Don will never forget.

The English Prime Minister, Winston Churchill dispatched all manner of boats, personal as well as commercial to help with the evacuation of over 330,000 men. This was a momentous undertaking, but God was apparently on their side. As my mother remembers, during the evacuation, the English Channel—usually windy, choppy and dangerous—was uncharacteristically calm.

On September 4, 1940, Don married his sweetheart Vera Jackson during the height of the Battle of Britain. I love to tell this story about their honeymoon. As they were on the train, bound for Exeter for their honeymoon, the rail line was bombed. The train itself sheltered in a tunnel and was delayed by hours. Don and Vera had only wedding cake to eat, which her bridesmaids had thoughtfully packed for them.

Upon arriving at Exeter, they were escorted through rubble and bombed-out streets to find their hotel. Don and Vera had brought bicycles for their trip, and spent their days bicycling and exploring Dartmoor, staying at farmhouses along the way. From one farmhouse they sent a postcard to Vera's family. Ordinarily, they would have continued on, but this particular farmhouse was especially amenable. So they returned there a few days later, to find the local police waiting for them!

Unbeknownst to them, the police had been on their trail. When I heard this story, I thought maybe Don had been considered AWOL, but Vera corrected me. His unit had ordered his immediate return on account of the imminent German invasion. The postcard sent to Vera's family was clearly marked with the postmark, Widecombe in the Moor. "That postcard was our undoing," says Don.

While Don was away at war, Vera maintained the home front. When the V1 bombs were raining down and war was raging, she volunteered for night shift nursing and also tended to their son, Derek. One day, walking the baby in his pram, Vera heard the ominous chugging sound of one of the bombs. She jumped into a ditch by the side of the road, turned the pram upside down over the baby and crawled under it. The bomb exploded in a field next to them. A farmer came out to help Vera and the baby out of the ditch. It was an amazing escape, but I'm sure Derek is a little tired of hearing this story being retold.

Then in 1943, Don was commissioned into the Royal Army Service Corps. He served from the beaches of Normandy on into Berlin, rising to the rank of Captain. He told me that he had been in the ruins of the Reich Chancellery building and had sat on the marble desk formerly belonging to Hitler. He was also in Hitler's Bunker and personally saw the pits where supposedly Hitler and Eva's bodies were burned. Years after the war, I realized what a significant event this would have been.

Having Don and Vera reveal their part in all of this history, showed me the strength of character of these two. I felt honored that they had shared their many experiences with me.

PATRIOTISM

Here is more evidence that World War II influenced many people's lives and shaped their opinions years later. One of my customers, an elegant, well-dressed man got excited one night when I mentioned mango sorbet as an offering for dessert. "Mango! Mango!" he said, "I grew up in the Philippines. My parents were working over there. I haven't had mango in a long time!"

He told me a little about living in the Philippines as a child. He was about five or six years old when World War II broke out. He said life was very difficult for his parents and other Americans who were overseas, and that the war took a huge toll on them. They were transferred from place to place, and had to endure great hardships and deprivation. I was touched when this man finished his narrative with, "We somehow lived through it."

He found himself sailing under the Golden Gate Bridge with his parents and a few survivors in 1945. He said that as a boy, he didn't understand why the adults were crying—it was a nice enough bridge, but what were all the tears about?

My customer said that the experience taught him what it means to live in a free country like the United States. He had witnessed firsthand what it can be like without the unique protections afforded us by our Constitution. He doesn't want anyone to take our freedoms or responsibilities for granted. He told me that he often tells his grandchildren the story and quizzes them on civics and the US Constitution.

CHAPTER SEVEN

Unusual Places & Characters

The Haunting of The Hilltop

The old house was built in 1892 as a residence for a dentist. It had seen service as a restaurant in the 1940s, a club house in the 1960s, and in 1979 it became an upscale restaurant, The Hilltop, that stayed in business until 2008. I started working there in 1990. The menu printed the history of the place, including the fact that it had once been a bordello. Actually, many old houses on the main route north out of San Francisco claimed that distinction. I suppose it added old world charm.

An elderly gentleman, very dapper with red suspenders, came into the restaurant one day. He was a distinguished Superior Court Judge. After this gentleman had dined at our place, he sent us a formal letter. The letterhead was official: Superior Court of Marin County, and the letter asked us to 'cease and desist' the claim that the restaurant was once a bordello because he, the Judge himself, had been the lawyer for the place years before, and had it been a bordello, he would have known! We took the claim off the menu, but still mentioned it to customers.

There was a basement in the building that we used as storage for wine, extra tables and chairs, and all the holiday decorations. There were five separate rooms, with an old bathroom at the end of the hall. I often thought to myself that had it been a bordello, this would have been a perfect set-up.

What we didn't mention on the menu was that the place may have been haunted. The house had an unfinished attic space with small dormer windows. Leaning against the walls were old black and white photographs of the town and its founders. The faces in the photos were a little scary and they gave the attic a spooky feeling. I used to take the new employees up the creaky stairs to show them around the place. The little tour meant that the staff had accepted 'the new guy.'

One time, I went up into the attic through the stairway off the kitchen. The cooks closed the door and locked it behind me. There I was, afraid of spiders, locked in the dark, spooky attic. I sat down on the stairs, closed my eyes and didn't make a sound. I knew they wanted me to scream and shout in fear. When I  made no noise, the cooks opened the door to see where I was. I came out, and told them that I would never go up into the attic again. It wasn't because I saw any ghosts or got any weird vibes. It was just dark and dusty.

One night a customer came out of the ladies room quite upset and wanted to leave even before she had eaten her dinner. The manager asked her what was wrong. The customer reported that she had heard a woman sobbing loudly in the next bathroom stall. Not knowing what would be appropriate, and being concerned as she listened to this poor woman crying, she finally called out, asking if there was anything she could do, and there was no answer. When the customer looked into the stall, there was nobody there. After listening to the story, the manager calmed the hysterical customer down, and persuaded her to stay for dinner.

Another time one of the cooks arrived early in the morning. He had no key for the place, so he crawled into a small basement area under the kitchen to rest and wait for the manager. As he was quietly waiting, he heard someone walking around the kitchen above him and assumed that the chef had arrived and had gone in unnoticed. When the cook climbed the stairs, the door was locked as before and no one was there.

But it was one particular night that things got interesting. It was my job to go down to the storage basement to replace wine that had been sold that day. I took a young waiter with me as we had about four cases of wine to bring up. We unlocked the basement, loaded three cases onto a dolly and I was carrying an extra case. As we locked up and started across the parking lot to go back into the restaurant, I found myself slipping forward, almost tripping, sort of running, and then I fell! The case of wine went flying forward. Not a bottle broke, and I landed on my back. How did I do that? The young man with me asked me why I tried to race him, and what a funny little turn I did when I fell. I couldn't explain it and thought that maybe I had tripped over something. When I checked the pavement, there was nothing that could have caused me to do the strange little dance.

We went into the restaurant and told everyone what had happened. As we were telling the story, the kitchen door swung open and another waiter came out, carrying a large tray laden with five or six dinner plates. All of a sudden, one of the waiter's legs 'curved' around the other one. He fell, and all the dinner plates went with him. What a mess! All eyes were on him. The waiter's girlfriend was visiting that night, sitting at the bar, and was of course watching his every move. She asked him why he had wrapped his leg around the other one. So, I wasn't crazy, I had seen the same thing!

We all figured it was the ghost acting up. I got off easy, a fall that left no bruise and no broken bottles. The other waiter had to apologize to his customers, who had to wait for their dinners to be prepared again. The legend was cemented that night and we all believed!

KITCHEN QUIPS

A lovely woman smugly told the chef once that she could make better soup. He answered, "Yes, but can you make it for 200?"

❧❧❧

The kitchen door swings open. A customer stands there obviously wanting someone's attention. We all turn towards him, when he calls out, "My steak wasn't as good as last time." The chef is on the spot. Stillness is in the air as we all anticipate what the chef could possibly say to placate this customer.

The Chef doesn't miss a beat, and calmly answers, "That cow is gone!" Satisfied, the customer nods his head in understanding, closes the door and leaves.

THE WEALTHY COUPLE

You could tell they were a wealthy couple by the different mink coats she wore, and the fact that their housekeeper came with them for dinner. But something seemed amiss. Under her mink coat, she was always underdressed, in housecoats and sneakers. Another unusual habit was that the wife and the housekeeper sat at one table, and the husband sat at another. They didn't seem to be fighting, it was just their way.

The Chef didn't like to see them because they were early diners, usually the first ones to arrive at the restaurant. He had been there since the morning, preparing the soup and his sauces. His only time to rest before the evening rush was just before we opened, when he could sit down to enjoy his meal. When these folks came in, he had to cut his break short and cook for them.

The couple always ordered a $15 New York steak to take home after they ate. It was for their dog! It was supposed to be done just medium rare. Sometimes they complained that the dog thought his steak was overcooked. In turn, the Chef complained to us about cooking for their dog. Maybe he overcooked the steak on purpose. They were good tippers, and aside from annoying the Chef, they were pleasant to wait on. All of the wait staff vied for their attention.

The husband wasn't supposed to drink any alcohol. When their meal was finished, he would pay for everything, make sure the steak was ready for the dog, and then order his wife to leave the restaurant with the housekeeper. He made sure the ladies were in the parking lot and on their way to the car. Out of view of his wife, the husband slowly walked past the bar, where the bartender handed him a shot of whiskey. He downed it without missing a beat, then went out to drive the ladies home. This went on for years, a few times a week. Even later on, when the husband walked with a cane, he still made sure he had his drink on the way out. He kept his arrangement with the bartender.

On occasion, the husband's brother came in with them. With unkempt white hair, dressed in T-shirts and wrinkled pants, he looked a little crazy. The family apparently had a lot of money in silver mines in Nevada. As the brother told me, the wealth made him 'eccentric, not crazy'. He lived in the penthouse suite in one of the fancy hotel/casinos on Lake Tahoe.

When the husband died, his brother came in to tell me. I was sad because he was unusual in his habits, but a decent man. To commemorate the occasion, the brother sat down to dinner by himself and ordered a bottle of champagne with two glasses. He drank half the champagne and left it on the table for the evening. Everyone wondered why the table was set that way, and I told them that this customer's brother had passed away, and the champagne was an offering for him. The evening went on, and even though I truly love champagne, I never touched it. After all, it was for someone else.

I never saw the wife or the housekeeper after that, but the eccentric brother stopped by a few times over the years. I always treated him well, even though he looked uncared for, almost homeless. I assume he's passed away by now. I hope someone gave him an honorable send-off just as he had done for his brother.

TREE MAN

One of my customers works for a tree service. He refers to himself as the 'branch manager.' Over the years, he told me a lot of jokes, but one in particular was appropriate. When I tell this to my customers, I usually warn them that it doesn't start out as a very funny joke:

A man was driving with his wife and she had a heart attack. The man called 911, and explained that his wife had suffered a heart attack. The 911 operator asked where the man was located, and he explained that he was on Eucalyptus. The operator asked if he could spell Eucalyptus, and the man said, "Just a minute. I'll drive her over to Oak."

INFORMATIVE MAN

Another neighbor was extremely forthcoming about his colorful life. We knew him before he was married, and he was somewhat of a lady's man. Since this behavior didn't change with marriage, we often heard of his exploits. He wasn't bragging, it was more informational and matter of fact.

He told us once of being stopped by a Highway Patrolman after he had left the bar. This was in the more lenient days. As part of the interrogation, the officer asked my neighbor to step out of the car and perform some tasks to prove sobriety, one of them being able to stand on one leg for a period of time.

The Officer was being patient, and explained repeatedly how to do it, trying to give our friend a break. Finally, our friend, tired of failing the exercise, blurted out, "It's easy for you! You haven't been drinking!" Needless to say, we heard about this at the bar and saw the resulting ticket.

He once gave me a lucky silver quarter. It was an early one, from 1944. He told me to keep it for him. I kept it in my waitress apron. Every once in a while he asked me to produce it, just to see if I actually still had it. Then he found another one stamped 1964, and gave me that one also. When he was in the restaurant, he often called out to me, "Show us your pair!" and I'd pull out these quarters. One weekend he was going to Reno to gamble and I tried to give him the lucky quarters. He refused, saying they were now mine, to bring me good luck.

Working in the construction business, my friend found yet another silver quarter, dated 1935, when he was pulling up an old wooden floor. That one was added to my collection. The 'Show us your pair' phrase had to be revised but I am still asked to produce the lucky quarters.

This neighbor had interesting siblings, six of them and we heard all about their comings and goings. Two of his sisters are gay. He once told me that his son likes to play with trains, and his daughter likes to play with dolls. He explained that in his family, this could be an issue!

I made everyone laugh one day when he and his sister were at the bar discussing which one of them would have the privilege of taking me home. All his buddies listening heard me say, "I'm sorry, but I have to go with your sister on this one!" I didn't go home with anyone. I have been happy with my man for many years, and everyone knew that, so it was doubly amusing.

My informative customer and I are still friends because of the length of time we've known each other, he says, way before I decided to go with his sister. The culmination of all this was one day when I heard him exclaim, "If you don't know everything about my life, you just haven't been listening!"

CHAPTER EIGHT

Remarkable Customers

WHAT A WOMAN!

This lovely woman was always very youthful, with smooth skin and dark hair. When she was younger, she had starred with the Ice Capades. She later married and had a family and was very proud when her daughter followed in her footsteps. I used to hear the stories when mother and daughter went to the Ice Capades reunions together.

When I first met this beautiful lady, I was surprised to find out that she was old enough to have grown children, she looked so young to me. She had a close family, two sons, a daughter and a devoted husband. Hawaii was a favorite place and her family vacationed there often.

Theater life was in this lovely lady's blood; she loved to talk about 'showbiz'. She had worked in the wardrobe department and her husband did the theater lighting. They often told me stories about working with different celebrities.

Getting to know this couple, watching their family grow, get married and have children was not that different from other customers, but I did feel closer to them. Like many other families, they spent consecutive holidays with us at the restaurant. I am privileged to watch the evolution of people's lives.

I was extremely sad and shocked when I found out that this very youthful grandmother had passed away quite suddenly. Her husband told us the remarkable story of her passing. It was right after Thanksgiving. She had just returned from a little trip, spending time with all her family. Uncharacteristically, she asked her husband to put up the Christmas decorations early. He asked why, and she said she wanted to enjoy them longer this year. So, the garlands went up on the fireplace, the tree was lit and hung with ornaments collected over the years, and the angels were in their places. Never before had the decorations looked so pretty.

That fateful afternoon our lady went shopping, one of her favorite pastimes. She came home and presented her husband with a gift, a little carved duck. She told him that she felt a little tired and sat down while he made her something to eat. When he came back out to the room, she was gone. Just like that! Needless to say, her husband cherishes that little duck, it now rides with him in his car.

Christmas came as usual. The family would have never had the heart to decorate for Christmas, but she saw to it that it had been done. They felt surrounded by her throughout the holiday because of her thoughtfulness.

She had always done all the shopping, even buying her husband's clothes. When I commented on the nice ensemble of shirt and sweater he wore, he said she had chosen it for him. They drove a really cute car, a Mini Cooper painted with a British flag. His wife had picked it out, of course. After she passed away, he was astonished to find the car was a 'chick magnet', although he wasn't interested.

Around the house, this lovely lady had always done everything. Her husband told me that he literally did not know how to operate the washing machine. She was so organized that when he started looking around the house, he found folders with operating instructions, warranties, date of purchase, receipts, all in place and accessible. Amazing! He told me months after her passing that he kept finding things taken care of. It was almost as if she had prepared, maybe not herself, but those around her.

I went to her funeral, a lovely church service, and her family came to the restaurant for dinner afterwards. She was cremated and her family spread her ashes in all her favorite places. They even took some to Hawaii and left part of her there. She was a beautiful person and I was glad to have known her. All I can say is, "What a woman!"

BIG AND BEAUTIFUL

One of my customers was a big, beautiful woman. Impeccably dressed, always manicured, with a gorgeous face. She often modeled for big and tall women clothing shows in San Francisco, but was always worried about her weight.

She was married to a wonderful French man who adored her and that's how I met her, when they came together to the restaurant. I got to know her and it turned out that we had gone to the same college. She was a few years before me, but her reputation was indelibly marked on the campus.

You see, the campus had a bell tower that usually played the ubiquitous Big Ben chimes. Until one day, when surprisingly, Jimi Hendrix came screaming through the PA system just as the clock chimed noon!

Everyone was talking about who had the nerve and guts to climb the bell tower to change the tape, and here I find out, years later that it was this lovely friend of mine! "You? You were the famous one with Jimi Hendrix?" We became friends after that.

One day she came in and said that she was on a diet. This particular diet did not allow food, and she was ingesting only vitamins and Diet Coke, with that poison aspartame. She was very excited and told me that she had lost 80 pounds! I was worried about her, but she told me that she was under the care of physicians in a local hospital–shame on them, in my opinion.

Time went by, but after the extreme strict diet, her body reacted by adding more weight when she started eating normally. So much so, she appeared noticeably larger than ever, as so often happens with these crash, starvation diets.

Sadly, this beautiful woman's heart gave out and she passed away in the middle of the night. She was 35 years old. When I saw her husband afterwards, he was devastated.

Interestingly enough, one time a few years after my friend's death, her husband was in the bar with some friends who were ogling a nudie magazine. He showed no interest whatsoever until they turned to a page full of Big and Beautiful women, and he actually leaned forward to look.

I wished that my friend had been there to see that. Her husband loved her just the way she was.

"I'M NOT 21"

A friendly couple started frequenting our establishment. These folks certainly liked to drink. When they dined at the restaurant, it was a full experience; having cocktails first, lunch or dinner, and then returning to the bar for after-meal refreshments. They came prepared, hiring a taxi for the ride to and fro.

I could always tell when they were planning to stay and get inebriated because their clothes betrayed them. As both were office workers, they usually wore business attire. So, the first time they came in dressed in rather funky sweat suits, I was surprised. The man asked if their clothing was acceptable, since they wanted to be more comfortable. With some apprehension, I acquiesced. After that, the same sweat suits were worn more and more.

When the couple stayed those lengthy afternoons and evenings, we did quite a bit of chatting and got to know each other. They were good for the house, in other words, spent a lot of money, polishing off most of a bottle of scotch and tipping generously.

A funny story about these customers came about one afternoon when they walked in, casually dressed, letting us know they meant business. They normally drank a particular brand of scotch. That day we only had a half bottle in our inventory. It was early in the afternoon and it appeared that we did not have enough to keep their whistles wet for very long. I asked the Chef what could be done since it was obvious that someone needed to go to the liquor store and get another bottle.

The only staff present were the bartender, the Chef, a young dishwasher and me. I asked the dishwasher if he was 21, and he said no, he wasn't 21. I asked the Chef, but he literally had the soup on and said he couldn't leave. I had to get the restaurant open, so I couldn't go and the same for the bartender as we were expecting a crowd.

As we were all discussing what we were going to do, the dishwasher kept saying that he would go. I reminded him that he had told me that he wasn't 21. We burst out laughing when he said, "I'm not 21, I'm 22!" So the 22-year-old dishwasher left and came back with a bottle of the preferred scotch. The couple, unaware of all the shenanigans, stayed, spent money and everyone was happy.

ORCHIDS AND LILIES

*"The party arrived in a white limousine,
bearing orchids and lilies, a sight to be seen..."*

This is the opening to a poem that I wrote to thank my very gracious customers for a grand and memorable Saturday night. They were a flamboyant and affluent couple who wanted everyone to share their good fortune. They had no children of their own but were very generous to many people, providing support and influence. Their house was always open to friends: good times, parties, football afternoons, any excuse for get-togethers. They had a beautiful garden at home, and once gave me a rose bush, which flourishes today in my back yard.

Coming to the restaurant was always a big deal. The couple

would call ahead for just two or three, but usually arrived with larger parties, in a limousine or with a driver. Flowers would arrive the afternoon before, corsages for the guests and the waitresses, too. The dinner turned into a grand occasion. The drinks at the bar were plentiful, before and after dinner. The couple tipped exorbitantly, over the top. They always made a splash and left a wake!

This flamboyant man once told me about a helicopter ride he took to search for property to buy in Northern California. He had the pilot land in a field in an area that looked promising. He found the local bar, took the pilot and the real estate agent in with him and bought drinks for all the patrons the whole day. The little town knew he was there!

This couple hosted infamous Christmas parties. They booked an upscale restaurant for a Saturday night, and hired three limousines to run back and forth bringing guests and taking them home. I attended three of these amazing parties. Part of the fun during the party was taking a ride in the limousine, just to go and come back.

A flower arranger was on hand with orchids for all the ladies. The parties got wild with conga lines snaking through the restaurant to lively music. And the party wasn't complete until the festive and erotically clad Santa's Helpers started losing their little outfits.

An open bar was just the thing to allow guests to take advantage of the limo service. I witnessed some of the guests order three or four drinks, just sip once, then leave them and order more. I told my host afterwards that if everyone had to pay fifty cents or a dollar for a drink, they wouldn't be so wasteful. He wouldn't even consider it. He wanted it to be lavish and extravagant. Cost was simply not an issue.

This generous and fun-loving couple ultimately bought some land up north to start a winery. They needed a label for their winery and held a contest. I have some artistic training in drawing still life: trees and bottles. Here was a chance to draw trees on bottles! I submitted a few drawings for the wine label, and won! They awarded me a check for $1000.

At that time my father was ill and wasn't going to live much longer. I was able to show my Dad my winning wine label. One of my father's friends had given me the art lessons many years before. He happened to be visiting my father at that time and was able to see that his former student had accomplished something positive with the training that I had received.

I was very happy and proud to share my lovely design of trees and a small stream running through a rocky arch with my Dad and my art teacher. But I will never see the label on any wine bottle. Shortly afterwards, my friends had to sell their winery to pay off back taxes to the IRS. I was concerned, but they didn't seem to be. I remember the man told me, "Darling, you expect these things when you don't pay your taxes."

Life went on as usual for the couple, but the dream of owning a winery was still in their heads. A few years later, they moved to another state to be near her mother. I kept in contact with them through Christmas cards, and they would come to the restaurant whenever they were in town. It's been years, but I still have customers ask, "Hey! Whatever happened to those people who had those fabulous parties?"

Happily, the latest Christmas card arrived with the news that land had been bought, grapes were planted, and the dream was coming to fruition. I don't expect my label to be used, as they have a different name for this winery. They'll probably hold another contest for the label, as it is a very cost effective way of getting an original label.

I'm also sure that this couple has another group of friends in their new area and their parties are still making waves. So the legend will continue.

Golf Buddies

She was 36, and he was 72. He was widowed, and she had never married. She was an accomplished musician and music teacher. They also both played golf and made a very good twosome. They came to dinner together after golf to discuss strategies and outcomes, and took turns paying for dinner.

Then one night I noticed that they were speaking a little more softly, a little more intimately. I had to put the candles out on the tables, but I didn't want to interrupt their quiet conversation. I was lighting and distributing candles on all the other tables, carefully avoiding theirs.

She called me over and said, "They have a candle, and they have a candle." Pointing around the room, she continued, "They have a candle, and even that table over there has a candle. So where's our candle?" I apologized profusely, and told them that they looked like they didn't want to be disturbed.

As it turned out, besides golf, this couple both had fantastic collections of Frank Sinatra in common, and were going to each other's houses to hear their stereo systems. It was clear that things were turning romantic.

The golf buddies ended up getting married. His family was extremely happy for him. He had someone to share his interests, and to be with him. She stayed with him until he passed on to the big golf course in the sky.

THE ADVENTURES CONTINUE

After the war, life went on for my friends Don and Vera. They usually dined at the restaurant on Tuesday evenings on their way home from San Francisco where Vera had her hair done. I reserved their favorite table #16 for them near the corner.

Don had made a name for himself with his study of windmills. He photographed over 1300 mills in all states of repair in England, and has a master collection of 5000 photos overall. He told me that because of his expertise, he had been consulted in 1954 in West Sussex County when there was a study to preserve three of the twenty-six windmills in the county.

When they first met, Don bought Vera a bicycle. On their honeymoon, and for years after, they continued with cycling. They rode all over Britain studying windmills for Don and satisfying Vera's interest in collecting photos of unusual and ornate post boxes. Her collection now includes photos I took when I went to Italy in 2001: an interesting mailbox in the Vatican, as well as a gorgeous bronze plaque with a collection aperture that I saw on a door in Northern Italy.

I asked them why they ever left England, because they appeared to be the epitome of a proper English couple. Don told me that in 1956, he realized that he had limited opportunities in England. He was quoted in the local newspaper, "I have got to the top of my little sapling". He decided to quit his well-paying and pensioned position, pick up his wife and son and make an audacious move across the Atlantic to Canada for opportunity and adventure.

Canada turned out to be a bit more difficult than first imagined. It was Vera who first got a job as a shorthand typist, while Don endured 88 interviews! Don finally ended up with a position at Avro Aircraft Company. Avro was famous for unveiling the first Canadian Supersonic Jet in March 1958. It was called the

Arrow, but was discontinued less than a year later. He became unemployed again in 1959 when Avro lost a bid to an American aircraft company. 56,000 men lost their jobs in one day.

How did they get to California, to meet me all these years later? The story continues. Don and Vera then had to make a decision, either to stay in Canada, go back to England...or somewhere else! They packed their car, with all their belongings and son Derek, and headed for California to become our neighbors and friends.

Over the years, I have met their son Derek, his lovely wife Hanny, and their children. I was lucky enough to be invited to Don and Vera's 65th wedding anniversary party, and helped them celebrate when Vera, then Don a year later, turned ninety years young. Vera is a wonderful baker and made her own grand cakes for these occasions.

Don and Vera spend a lot of time in their garden that has been cultivated with real English primroses and bluebells, and is lovely the year round. The garden is designed to invite reflection, complete with rock walls, winding paths, little nooks with benches, and flowers climbing on trellises. When I visit, it feels like I'm in a little English park. They do all the upkeep themselves. We just have to keep Don off the ladder, because he likes to paint the whole house himself. After all he's been through, to him it's just another of life's little chores.

VIP GUESTS

One restaurant had an absentee owner, the money man, who did not have much to do with the day to day running of the place. He was a business man well known in the county with other restaurants to his name. When he did come in to eat, he was treated as a VIP. Most of the time I was his server. Sometimes he dined alone, but when he brought guests they were important people: other business owners in the area, bankers and high-ranking local politicians. Even though we kidded around privately, I was very professional when he had these business meetings...usually.

One day this boss arrived early and told me that this luncheon was very important. A State Senator would be joining him for a meeting, and he wanted everything to go smoothly. This particular State Senator had a reputation for being rude. After bringing drinks to the table, non-alcoholic of course, I asked the Senator what he would like for lunch. He said that he wanted a Chicken Salad. I responded that we had three chicken salads on the menu, and started to list them: "Chicken Caesar..." This famous man, now impatient with me, interrupted rather loudly, "If I wanted Chicken Caesar, I would have asked for Chicken Caesar!" I couldn't help myself. I blurted out, "Good, then that narrows it down to two!" I think I intimidated the Senator because he then lowered his voice and ordered Chinese Chicken Salad. I was a little worried about my boss' reaction, but I continued, took the rest of the order and served their lunch.

I anticipated some repercussion afterwards but there was no fallout from this encounter. Apparently the Senator is used to speaking rudely and being spoken to in the same manner.

CHAPTER NINE

Famous Pets & Infamous People

Resident Cats

The cat lived at the restaurant for many years. He showed up one day as cats do, and liked the place. Large and darkly mottled, the cat lived outside, roaming the parking lot and sleeping behind the building near the warm outlets of the laundry room. The boss said it was good to have a cat on premises, to keep mice from taking up residence. In the morning when the Chef's car arrived, the cat came out. When the Chef went home at night, the cat retired to his spot. He and the Chef understood each other.

The Chef had an old plastic milk crate just outside the kitchen door where he sat during restful moments, and the cat sat next to him. I should have taken a photo of the two of them to retain the memory.

He wasn't a friendly cat. He didn't like to be petted. When a customer approached him, he would open his mouth like a lion ready to roar, but never made a sound. The sight of his little teeth usually made the customers leave him alone. He only needed one friend, the Chef.

The restaurant was famous for homemade liver pate. Baked in loaves, we sliced it for the hors d'oeuvres. Any small remnants went into a bowl. When I was new at the restaurant and did not yet understand the procedures, I spotted that bowl of pate, perfectly good, quite inviting and helped myself. The Chef calmly said, "You're eating the cat's food."

Besides the pate, the cat was treated to morsels. The Chef liked to play a game with him. He stood with his back to the door, his fist closed around a treat, a piece of beef, chicken, or fish, and then surprised the cat by tossing it out to him.

On rainy days, the cat sat just outside the kitchen door under the roof overhang. Once in a while, he sneaked over the threshold and sat inside. The Chef would see him, point outside and quietly say, "Hey, hey." The cat would then step back outside. He knew where he was supposed to be.

Ultimately, the cat got old, and wasn't doing so well. One of our customers was a veterinarian affiliated with UC Davis, not far from us. He took the cat to his hospital for treatment. We all missed the cat, especially the Chef.

A few weeks later, the doctor called and told us that the cat had passed away. We were all worried because we had been eating the same diet as the cat: rich pate and lovely sauces. Fearing the cat may have had heart or cholesterol problems, we breathed a sigh of relief when the doctor informed us it was respiratory failure. The rich food didn't hurt the cat and he had lived a good life at the restaurant. I still enjoy the pate, and so does the doctor!

Another cat arrived on scene. He moved into the house next door and quickly figured out that there was a restaurant serving food nearby. He was a large, orange tabby named Sparky and started visiting every day. His owner was a nine year old girl who often came looking for him.

Sparky often snuck into the restaurant and maneuvered under the tables. He knew that if found, he'd be picked up and put outside. Once I put him out the front door, he came back in through the side door. Being put out again, he circled around and cleverly came back in through the rear door. He also begged at the tables. Being large enough to stand on his back legs, his head came just over the top of the tables. The customers found his actions cute, and were so enthralled, they rewarded him with food. I tried to pick Sparky up once, finding him heading for the tables. He dug his claws in and was lifting the whole carpet, so I had to put him back down. That time he got to stay.

The customers were getting to know Sparky. Once I apologized to a certain table because he kept running back to them, for some reason. They replied, "But, he loves the Mahi Mahi!"

His owners tried to keep him home. One day, I was standing at the kitchen door and I looked over at Sparky's house. I saw the cat come out of a second story window, cross over the roof, jump down a series of levels, and head for the restaurant. Another time, I saw him climb over and squeeze through the lattice wood frame surrounding the porch. He was bound and determined to come to us.

We set the patio tables for lunch. On the sunny days, Sparky chose a table, climbed up and proceeded to stretch out. He used his feet to knock the silverware onto the floor. So that table was lost to us for the lunch shift!

Some of the customers complained about a health hazard, having a cat in the restaurant. Others said there was nothing to worry about, and complained about the complainers. I have to admit we had a hard time keeping him out since the doors to the restaurant were usually open.

Unfortunately, Sparky was a little too confident, and crossed the road one too many times. We mourned him. The little girl was devastated. Her mother got her another orange tabby and she named him Sparky. She keeps this one in the house.

RALPH THE DOG

It wasn't always cats that visited the restaurant. Ralph was a big black lab, who lived a few houses away. His owners walked down quite regularly to sit outside on the patio. Ralph joined them for dinner. He knew when it was time to come because he got a red bandanna around his neck. He walked very proudly with his neckerchief, and understood that he had to be a good dog.

Ralph knew the routine. He would obediently go under the outside table, and lie down. Most of the customers didn't even know he was there. His owners would order a child's plate for him. Usually a hamburger, in reality, it was a chopped sirloin, a pretty fancy hamburger for a dog.

I asked the Chef if it was all right, because the owners put the plate down for Ralph, just as it came from the kitchen, vegetables and all. The Chef said the dog's mouth was cleaner than most peoples' mouths. And, of course, the dish always went into the dishwasher afterwards.

I never told my boss that Ralph was the one getting the child's plate. The Chef knew and didn't seem to care. I don't know if the boss knew, but as business goes, a sale is a sale.

FAMOUS RADIO MAN

My boss, Roger, has a long-time friend who is a well-known radio show host. This gentleman and his wife frequent the restaurant, and it is especially nice when Roger can sit down and spend time with them. They have all known each other for thirty years. The Radio Man often mentioned our restaurant on the radio, although never by name, but my friends called me, saying that they had heard he had been there.

The Radio Man usually comes in with a hat on and his collar pulled up, trying to remain incognito, and sits in the back room alone, as his voice is so recognizable. On occasion, he brings his little dog. The dog sits on the chair beside him and is treated to a hamburger, well done, with no seasoning, the way the dog likes it. One time, they brought the dog, and he was sitting on his chair as usual. The Radio Man told me that the dog had already eaten and he wouldn't be getting his hamburger. The dog heard this, cocked his little head and whimpered. We all erupted in laughter and the dog got his hamburger.

The biggest event with this famous man was when I lost his credit card! He gave me the card and at the same time asked for a To Go bag, which I had to get in the kitchen. I didn't want to leave the card unattended near the credit card machine, so I took it with me into the kitchen.

It disappeared. Just like that! Vanished from its little tray! What do I do? Honesty is the best policy, so I went to the Radio Man and told him that I had just lost his card. He was very nice about it and started looking in his pockets saying maybe he hadn't given it to me.

But he had given it to me, and I had lost it! I panicked. I looked everywhere! Just inside the kitchen door was a big laundry bag with all the dirty tablecloths. The boss, now aware of what was going on, screamed at me, "Of all the people! He can ruin us!" and then pitched into the dirty linen, going through everything. No card.

I went back out to the famous customer, who was waiting to leave with his driver. I told him that we hadn't found it. He was so nice about it. He said, "Look at you! So nervous over a piece of plastic. Don't worry, I'll cancel it when I get home." His voice was so calm, I almost started to feel better. Then he said, "My wife's gonna freak!" I thought, Oh dear! Oh dear me!

The Radio Man told me that I would probably find it five minutes after he left, so he and the driver went out to the parking lot to the car. I went into the kitchen, heaving a huge sigh of disappointment. As I relaxed and stepped back, there was the card, to the left of me on the floor, hiding under a little shelf. It had apparently aeroplaned a few feet. I grabbed the card and rushed into the restaurant, just as the driver was coming back in.

The To-Go bag had leaked and he was coming back in to get it rewrapped. With great relief, I handed the card to the driver.

I still see the Radio Man. We're friends now, and I even asked him for an autograph for my aunt and uncle. We never mention the incident, and I hope he never told his wife.

INFAMOUS MOVIE DIRECTOR

One night in the restaurant, I was waiting on a large party. It was all one big family, with a distinguished white haired man at the head of the table. All went well, and at the end of the evening, the man handed me his credit card to pay for the meal. I thought that I recognized his name.

It was slightly different, but close enough, to a local adult film director. I took a big risk by mentioning this when I returned his card to be signed. I said, "There's a movie director that has the same name as you." I had seen his movies in theaters and for rent. He was famous.

The family surprised me by yelling out, "That's him! That's our Dad!" I handed him one of the restaurant's business cards and asked him for his autograph. He graciously signed.

When I got home, I called my Mother, and told her whom I had just met. She answered with a familiar, yet unimpressed, "That's nice, dear."

Later, I was bragging about meeting this famous director at the bar. One of my customers mentioned that he, too, had met him. My customer worked for a telephone company and had installed a system of telephones at the director's house. The funny thing was that a few months after he had completed the job, he was at a bachelor party where some stag films were being shown. My customer was accused of watching the film a little too closely. He protested, "No, I'm not watching the action, those are the phones I installed!"

Years later, I was training new employees at another restaurant when I was introduced to a nice young man. Here again, I noticed the last name. I took another risk and asked this young man, who was nervous to be applying for a job, if he was related to the movie director. Yes, he was related. He was his son. I mentioned that I had met his Dad, and had asked him for his autograph.

"You! That was you?" Apparently, his family still talks about that dinner, how nice it was and how the waitress had recognized their Dad. The movie director has since passed away. Throughout all of this, nobody ever asked me how I knew of these movies. I like to keep a low profile, but let it be known that still waters run deep!

KITCHEN QUIP

After forgetting to bring items out to the table, and having to return to the kitchen a number of times, I was complaining about running back and forth. The Chef told me that if you don't use your brain, you'll have to use your legs!

CHAPTER TEN

Slightly Scandalous

I'm Engaged to This One

The evening was drawing to a close. It was getting late, and I was waiting for a table of two to finish. They had enjoyed a particularly romantic meal, Rack of Lamb for two, plus a bottle of expensive red wine, so I was reluctant to rush them.

After some time, I approached the table and interrupted. It was almost 11:00 and I told them I was leaving but the boss was still there, and for them to be comfortable and finish their coffee and dessert. Then I went home.

The next evening, I recognized the same lady as she and a different man got out of their car and began to enter the restaurant. She walked quickly from the car, got to the door before her date, and motioned for me to keep quiet. She whispered, "I'm engaged to this one!"

My eyebrows raised slightly, but otherwise I made no response. I showed them to the same table the romantic couple had occupied the night before. It was a perverse move on my part because there were plenty of other tables available. My new friend ordered Rack of Lamb again, and her fiancé mentioned that it was her favorite. Apparently!

The woman excused herself to use the ladies room, and discreetly requested that I join her. Ah, the bathroom confidential! She explained to me that yes, she was engaged, but that she had accepted the previous evening's offer to come to this out-of-the-way restaurant, where she was sure nobody would know her. Then her fiancé surprised her by bringing her this evening, explaining that he wanted to show her a new place. She told me that as they were driving and getting closer, she kept praying there were two restaurants along this road! I kept her confidence. I saw her again a few times afterwards, and learned that she had called off the wedding.

Fate had quietly explained to her that there were consequences to cheating, and she wasn't ready to settle down.

WHITE MINI SKIRT

A strikingly tall woman well over six feet walked into the restaurant. She was dressed in a white leather mini skirt, white vinyl boots—you couldn't miss her. All eyes followed her as she and her date sat down to have a drink and then order dinner.

After a while, she went to the ladies room and was in there for about 35 minutes. Meanwhile, her date finished his meal, paid for dinner and was waiting for her in the bar. He looked a little concerned. When I asked if everything was OK, the gentleman asked me to go into the ladies room and check on his date, as he's had women go out the window on him before. (!) I told him not to worry as there were no windows in the ladies room.

When I went in, I found the woman at the counter, standing in a sea of discarded paper towels and tissues. Each piece of paper was smeared with makeup, foundation and lipstick from numerous bottles spread about. I then realized I was looking at a transvestite in somewhat of a panic. Evidently, his makeup had been coming off, probably due to excess sweat, and he was obviously trying to repair the damage.

I made a few noises about the mess in the bathroom, and finally mumbled something to the effect of, "Your date's waiting." Then I went out to the bar and calmly announced, "She'll be right out."

A few minutes later, a restored, stunning woman emerged from the bathroom, took her date by the arm and with dignity, left the restaurant. I'm sure her date did not know, and neither did any of the other patrons, that she was not exactly as advertised.

WAS SHE PRETTY?

Two brothers were having dinner, a nice evening out, deciding to finish with Irish Coffees. Well, as is often the case with alcohol, one is good and two is better! They were feeling the effects of the alcohol, and it was apparent in their laughter and antics. Their dinner was finishing up when another couple came in and sat at a neighboring table. Like-minded and similarly intoxicated, the two parties befriended each other, sent over drinks and eventually all four were sitting at one table. The woman of the newly arrived couple seemed to be enjoying herself immensely and went from lap to lap, sort of being passed around. Then the kissing started.

At one point, one of the brothers got up from the table and staggered. He ended up stepping backwards and falling through a door, down a small stairway, actually landing into another dining room. Customers were startled to see this man fall into the room and got up to help this poor guy. The confused brother stood up, shook himself off and said to the helpful customers, "Where the f*** did you come from?" I was the only one laughing. He managed to get back to his brother who had been monopolizing the woman's attention, and it was apparently time to call it a night.

The man who had brought the woman in decided to take her home. He seemed to know the routine. He stood her up, which was a very unsteady proposition. Standing facing her, he bent down, putting his head between her legs, if you can picture this, and hoisted her hips over his shoulders, with her head hanging down his back like a sack of potatoes. His hands were holding onto her legs, which were sticking out in front of him and he used her feet to sort of push open the front door. Outrageous! And he carried her out to the car like that. The brothers sheepishly found their way home.

The next day, the same woman called the restaurant. "Someone told me that I was at the restaurant last night. Is my purse there?" I told her we had it and would keep it for her until she came for it. I know she came in and retrieved it, but I was not witness to her return to the scene of the crime.

One of the brothers came in the next night, sought me out and simply asked, "Was she pretty?"

My Husband's Out of Town

"Show me a husband who won't, and I'll show you a neighbor who will."   *--Comedian Redd Foxx*

One night a customer had had too much to drink, so we took his car keys away from him and called a taxi. When the taxi arrived, the man refused to go and the taxi left. The man stayed at the bar with his head down almost sleeping.

This was, of course, not a very good image for a dinner house. So the boss brought him some coffee, which he refused, and even some sandwiches, which were also refused. We were in a quandary, not knowing what was going on with this guy.

Half an hour later, in came a neighbor lady whom we all knew. She had obviously had a few belts and was in a sultry mood. Leaning against the door frame just inside the bar area, she paused and stood there for a few moments, getting everyone's attention. Sensuously running her hand through her hair, she softly announced, "My husband's out of town."

At that, the drunk guy's head popped up as if a switch had gone on. Within five minutes, he had offered her a place at the bar next to him and had bought her a drink, observing all the formalities. Then, all of a sudden he was escorting her out the door, presumably to her place. Remember, he had no car keys. I went straight to the bartender and with some surprise in my voice exclaimed, "I didn't know that they knew each other!" He responded, "What's the matter with you? They don't know each other! That guy didn't want another drink, he didn't want anything to eat, he didn't want a taxi. We know what he wanted!!"

I went home that night and recounted the event. Up until then I hadn't fully realized the implications of the phrase, "My husband's out of town."

THE SPOON STORY

A couple came in for dinner and were eating, drinking and enjoying themselves. The lady was dressed in a very revealing sundress, down to there and up to here, and boy, did she have the body to wear it! As they were eating, the scantily clad diner kept dropping her spoons under the table, and her date went down to retrieve them. The other waitress and I figured that he must have been blind. He was under the table for long periods, and at first we thought maybe he just couldn't find the spoons.

It wasn't that long before we figured out that he wasn't looking for the spoons. Apparently, the gentleman was enjoying himself under the table. Since we don't see these things everyday, both of us waitresses brought our dinners out to the buffet in the dining room and stood eating, looking like we were trying to mind our own business and yet not miss anything. The night was getting on and all the other tables had paid and left.

Soon the lady called me over to the table. I was nervous, thinking that she had caught on to our Peeping Tom activity, when she said, "Excuse me, but I'm out of spoons!" With that, the couple and I started laughing and talking. It was their first date and things were going well.

The happy couple went on to get married and came back six years later. She was a little surprised that I readily remembered them, but some things are not so easily forgotten. They were planning a big party for their sixth anniversary with both their families at the restaurant where they had their first date.

For the event, my peeping companion waitress and I were ready for them and set up a long table. We made a decoration with spoons all down the middle of the table: tea spoons, soup spoons, serving spoons. Some of the party kept asking, "What's with spoons?" We told them that we just wanted to insure that they never ran 'out of spoons'.

NOT FIT TO SERVE

The benefits of restaurant work usually include employee meals. Some are better than others. We employees were partaking one evening and commenting on how lucky we were to be having steak.

However, my steak was not particularly tender. I gathered up my nerve, went into the kitchen to comment...well, to complain. I said to the Chef that my steak was full of gristle. I acknowledged his expertise in the matter when he answered me, "Well, I certainly wasn't going to give that one to the customer!"

One night the employees were treated to something different. An unidentified main dish was set before us. When questioned, the Chef said, 'swimming duck'. I'm pretty good with cooking terms, and very knowledgeable about our restaurant's menu, but had never even heard of that one. It was duck, off the bone, in a rather dark wine sauce. It was edible, but not my favorite.

The explanation came later. The morning cook was in love and his girlfriend had been visiting him that day when he was supposed to be cooking the ducks. The cook had gone outside to chat, lost track of time and had burned everything. Here again, we couldn't serve these to the customers and they were relegated to the employees' table. Apparently a rich dark wine sauce was just the thing to cover up the taste.

SILLY CUSTOMERS

A lady wanted steamed vegetables, no butter. I said, "No problem." She repeated that the vegetables needed to be steamed, with no butter, and I again said, "That's really no problem."

Then she ordered her main course, which was Veal Picatta. I said, "Ma'am, that dish is made with a butter sauce." She said, "Oh, that's OK, I can have it with the veal, I just can't have it with the vegetables!"

One of my favorite 'customer on a diet' orders: Chicken with cream sauce, soup, salad, dessert and a DIET Coke!

CHAPTER ELEVEN

Life at the Bar

A Memorable New Year's Eve

This story is about problem drinking and is actually about me. It was New Year's Eve and my shift started at 5:00 PM. The evening bartender came on at the same time, and when we entered the restaurant together, the party was in full swing. This was a lady bartender. Her dad had taught her the art of mixology and she had honed her skills to perfection. She was proud of her profession. I ordered my first customers' round, which was four drinks. This particular night, just coming on, with a big crowd, she picked up the bottles and started pouring, not realizing that the previous bartender had a different arrangement of bottles.

Usually a bartender sets his bottles in just such a way as to automatically pour, especially on a busy night. So these first four drinks were two gins, a vodka and a scotch. She poured all four drinks, then noticed the 'scotch' was a different color. She realized they were all mistakes. Our lady bartender told me to take the four 'mistake' drinks to the dishwashers, and she'd rearrange her bottles and make the correct ones for me. On the way to the kitchen, I had a brainstorm. It's New Year's Eve! Why should the dishwashers get these? So I hid them away and proceeded to drink them one by one. It took me about an hour.

The last one, I remember was a scotch and tonic. I went out to the bar and loudly proclaimed, "I can't recommend that last drink!" Uh, oh! All eyes were on me. The lady bartender knew, and everyone else knew, that I had not given those drinks to the dishwashers. She exclaimed, "You drank all those!" I didn't have to answer. I was too busy dancing in the bar.

All the patrons turned their seats to watch me. I don't usually dance through the bar with my arms flailing gracefully. But the music was rousing and it was New Year's Eve! I was very happily waiting on my tables too, which were ordering more drinks than usual. Their waitress was unusually sympathetic.

Since I was still doing my job, the boss did not notice any abnormality. The evening's work was winding down so he offered us our usual New Year's Eve drink. I accepted, and later when the champagne was uncorked, I accepted again!

I was walking home in those days, and got home, very happy, about 1:00 AM. Now the next morning was a different story. I had the obligation to go in and open the restaurant for New Year's Day brunch. Who else but old reliable Linda could be counted on for not overindulging the night before. Well, just as I had professionally done my job the night before and gotten myself home, I showed up on time the next morning.

The Chef told me that he had never seen me look exactly like that before. I said, "Excuse my French, but I feel like s***!" The Chef said something about that not being French. I asked him what the soup was, and he told me the soup wasn't ready. I repeated "What's the soup?" There was obviously something in my inflection, and he caught on to my mood, so he answered that it was black bean soup. I desperately needed something to eat, so I ate the underdone black bean soup. It was the best soup I've ever had.

Working brunch turned out to be a trial. Standing at the tables was difficult, keeping the orders straight in my aching head was challenging, and none of the food smelled very good.

It was a fun New Year's Eve, a truly awful New Year's Day and a good story to tell. Now that I'm older, and have had the experience, I know that I will never celebrate the New Year in such a way ever again.

Not All Bartenders Are Gentlemen

I worked with one seasoned bartender for a few months. He was older, had been at the restaurant a few years and seemed to know his business. We actually lived in the same town. I was taking the bus back and forth at the time and one night he offered me a ride home in his car. Being mindful of saving pennies, I thought I'd save the bus fare and accepted the ride.

When we got out to the parking lot, he surprised me by opening up his car trunk. Inside was a full bar. Shelves folded open to reveal glasses, a full ice bucket, stir spoons, strainers, and many bottles of liquor. He said he never drove without a drink, and asked me what I wanted. I was sort of shocked and stood there for a while in silence, so he made the choice for me. Apparently we were having Stingers! That's half brandy and half crème de menthe, over ice. He fixed one for me and a large one for himself. Bringing the drinks into the car, off we went towards home.

It was about a twenty minute ride to our town. When we got close, I noticed that he turned off the highway a little early for me. I mentioned that this was not my exit. Oh, he knew that, but he thought that my accepting the ride and the drink meant I was going to his house. I said no, that I had somebody waiting for me at home.

Now this 'gentleman' was angry. He drove a little further, stopped the car in not the best part of town and told me to find my own way home! Here was a co-worker of mine, at least 15 years older than I, treating me like this! I found a phone booth, called a taxi, and paid four times the bus fare! Be careful of trying to save pennies.

I did see him at work afterwards. He avoided me, but let it be known it was my fault for leading him on. All I thought was that I had learned a good lesson, with a lucky escape.

Months later, this bartender told all the co-workers that he had bought some property in a secluded part of the state and was looking for investors for his neighborhood party group. I didn't volunteer.

A REAL GENTLEMAN

Another bartender was a hard worker and honest as the day is long. Our boss went out of his way to hire him. This bartender was commuting from far away, almost an hour's drive each way, but the boss wanted him. His professionalism was such that he had a good following. It was worth it monetarily for him to travel all that way.

The bartender's girlfriend sometimes drove the long distance to visit him. He didn't like that because he did not want her drinking and driving. She liked champagne. I often saw him pour her only a little champagne and a lot of ginger ale. He swore she couldn't tell the difference. His girlfriend was also a little clumsy and would often spill her drink. This embarrassed the bartender. It wasn't that she was drunk, she was just a little scatterbrained.

We found out that he had previously worked in Las Vegas and liked big jewelry. We never knew why, but he always carried a jewelry box in his pocket and if you asked him, he reached in and made a production of opening the box. There was usually a big ring, or a large jewel or pendant, each time showing us a different one. Maybe he put his money in such things as  investments, but I'd never seen a man who had such a collection.

When this bartender was younger he had worked in the Pacific Northwest in the lumber mills. His wife had died young and he raised four children, all sons, by himself. He used to say that when his children were first born, they only asked for milk, then they got older and asked for steak! He had lived a full life, understood people and could sympathize with their problems.

Sometimes he had no patience. I saw him once tell a man, as he was entering the bar, "Get out! Leave now, and tell all your friends not to come here!" We were shocked, because he was such a friendly bartender and to have him summarily dismiss a potential customer was quite out of the ordinary. He told us later that he knew the man, and had plenty of trouble from him in the past. We all took his word for it, and the man never returned.

We worked together about six years. Then this hard-working and well-liked bartender got sick. He had either black lung disease or mesothelioma. Apparently he got it from the lumber mill work when he was younger. He was in the hospital for a while. Then the doctors told him that they couldn't do anything more for him, so the bartender told the doctors that he would rather go home than stay in the hospital for his last days.

His girlfriend went to the hospital to bring him home. As they were driving, the bartender told her that he wanted to stop at his favorite bar. The girlfriend was horrified. "You are sick! You have to go home!" she said, but he insisted, and they stopped.

They were at the bar and my friend ordered a drink for himself, a glass of champagne for his girlfriend, and told a dirty joke about a nun. Just then, his head dropped down and his body slumped forward. His girlfriend reached over to him, spilling her drink as the noon siren rang out. My friend had died on his own terms.

In his will, he had left enough money for that particular bar to open for one day and offer food and drink to everybody. He was a class act all the way.

Even the Best Ones Slip

One bartender was a very careful man, meticulous about his bar and his personal things. He had a fancy sports car that he was very fond of. We hardly saw it. He bought it to go on weekend excursions with his wife. When he did bring it to work, he carefully covered it and often went out to the parking lot to check on it, to make sure nobody had parked too closely.

Therefore, I was surprised one afternoon, when I arrived early to open up the restaurant, and there was the fancy sports car, minding its own business, uncovered and vulnerable in the parking lot. The surprise turned to wonder when I heard Bruce Springsteen blaring from the bar.

It was early and we weren't open yet, but when I walked in, a very happy bartender greeted me. He was dressed unprofessionally in a flowered Hawaiian shirt, with only stocking feet! I couldn't help but notice. I looked around and saw a neighbor sitting at the bar, having a drink.

Usually this meticulous bartender would not serve drinks until we were open. The bar needed to be cleaned, arranged, and set up just so before he could serve anyone. He often made customers wait until the clock struck exactly opening hour. Yet, here was a very spirited bartender, a paying customer...and Bruce Springsteen.

The bartender said to me, "What are you drinking?" Not one to miss a chance such as this, I said, "I'll have a Fernet", which is my usual drink. I was poured a noticeably large drink which I took to the back to sip on casually. I asked the bartender what he had been doing all day. I was getting into the spirit myself. His response was that he had had a bottle of wine for breakfast!

Ah, it was all becoming clear to me now. We had a busy upcoming Saturday night, a restaurant to prepare, and as I stated, a very inebriated bartender. I went to the house phone and called our back-up bartender who lived next door. I quietly explained the situation and asked him if he could possibly fill in for the evening. He arrived promptly.

The rest of us came to work as usual. The night was busy, in fact a little busier than usual, as the patrons at the bar stayed a little longer to watch the entertainment. The back-up bartender worked normally, taking care of customers. The happy bartender occupied a small corner of the bar playing DJ, and hosting a crowd of onlookers. Business was good. The boss never came in that night. All the waiters pooled extra money for the back-up bartender plus he made his tips. He was happy and we all made a deal not to mention the incident to the boss.

Needless to say, as such things are wont to do, the story reached the boss, albeit a few years later. As far as I know, nothing was ever mentioned to our regular bartender. He's a great bartender and honest, and everyone is allowed an off day or two. As you may have noticed in my previous recollection, I am in no position to judge.

CHAPTER TWELVE

"I am a Waitress"

LONGEVITY

Being at the same restaurant for so many years, I got to know a lot of families. I watched their kids grow up. When the kids started dating, they would bring their dates out to dinner and tell them, "This waitress is a friend of my parents." That made me feel a little old.

Customers often ask me, "How long have you been here?" I try to be humorous by answering, "Since 5:00!" Then I tell them, 18, 20, 25, or 28 years. The time kept getting longer, since that is what time does, and the customers were often disbelieving, in fact, amazed.

I tell them my secret, "I show up on time, I don't steal and I'm not noticeably drunk!" Then one night I added to that resume. The boss had bought new little lights to put on the stairway. He was trying to find an appropriate place to plug them in when I showed him that the stairway had built-in outlets just for the purpose. He said, "You're a genius!"

So my resume increased to four items: I show up on time, I don't steal, I'm not noticeably drunk plus I know where all the light plugs are! Now that's job security!

HEIMLICH MANEUVERS

One day at the restaurant, the Health Department sent some instructors to teach us the Heimlich Maneuver. As they demonstrated this life-saving technique, I realized that it was a simple idea, yet before it became well known, many people lost their lives from choking.

The first time the lesson came in handy, I was surprised by how much information I had absorbed. When confronted with someone choking, there's just no time for wavering. I saw from across the room that the young woman sitting with her family suddenly couldn't breathe. I rushed right over to her. She stood up abruptly, and I got behind her and performed the Heimlich. A large piece of beef literally flew out of her mouth. She took a deep breath and gasped a sigh of relief.

I was rather shocked when her father just crossed his arms over his chest, and said condescendingly, "Heimlich Maneuver." I couldn't believe it! I had just saved his daughter's life, but the jerk didn't even thank me, and to add insult to injury, tipped under 15%!

The Chef congratulated me, and gave me a glass of wine to calm my nerves and stop my hands from shaking. He could see that it was an emotional ordeal for me, even though the family had not acknowledged it adequately. Let's face it, it's unusual for a waitress to have a customer's life in her hands.

LONG STRETCH

The second time I had the opportunity to execute the maneuver, it was a large woman who needed help. She was sitting at a round table having lunch. I saw she was in trouble and went to her. Because of her girth, I had a hard time getting my arms around her.

I just stretched my arms as far as I could, mumbled an apology for the familiarity as I squeezed her, and pulled. The food dislodged and she could breathe again. I don't remember what particular tidbit was the culprit at that time, but the lady was able to finish her meal and go about her day. She was thankful, but embarrassed. There's really no reason for her to be embarrassed. It can happen very quickly. A few moments of discomfort versus a loss of life!

CLOSE CALL

The third time I needed my Heimlich training, I was not successful. It was Thanksgiving Day and the restaurant was full. I was carrying a big stack of dirty dishes back to the kitchen when I spotted a woman in trouble.

I quickly looked around for a place to set down my load. There was nothing close by, so I put them on the floor and stepped behind the woman. As I was trying to find her diaphragm, I was panicked and distracted. All I could think of was the manager, a particularly tough gal, yelling at me for putting dirty dishes on the floor. Precious time was passing.

An angel whispered in my ear, "I'm a Paramedic" and I stepped back. He quickly got into position and saved the lady's life. The restaurant erupted into applause! The lady's table paid for the whole Thanksgiving Dinner for the Paramedic and his family.

I picked up the dishes and took them back to the kitchen. I'm always amazed at the inconsequential things that I worry about, but all turned out extremely well that Thanksgiving Day.

THE SUBJECT OF TIPPING

As a waitress, I make my living on tips. "I have always depended on the kindness of strangers." Blanche DuBois immortalized that phrase in the play *A Streetcar Named Desire* by Tennessee Williams. It pertains particularly to me. I'm sometimes astonished, and appreciative, how generous customers are. Therefore, I cannot complain when I get a smaller, yet heartfelt, tip.

Then there's the occasion when I don't get tipped at all. I have bad days, maybe forget something or say the wrong thing, and I don't deserve a tip, which is for courteous service. Tipping is not mandatory. A server has to earn their tips. My theory is that a waiter or waitress who doesn't do their job well, shouldn't be compensated, won't be happy and will therefore find another line of work. The other side is, when you're well compensated, like me, you can end up making a career of waiting tables.

One evening, an older gentleman was paying for his dinner when he mentioned to me that he remembered when the going rate of tipping was 10%. I nodded, and then he said, "...until the waiters decided to make it 15%!" He was apparently upset that he thought he had to leave a set amount. I answered that he could leave whatever he felt like, and that it was purely voluntary. Besides, I added, if the waiters had any say in the matter, we would have asked for 50%!!

❧❧❧

That particular gentleman would probably be surprised to find out that I haven't always left a tip! There are two instances that come to mind where I thought that a tip was not only unnecessary, but would have been wrong. I can't reward bad behaviors. The first instance occurred when my friend and I were at our favorite seafood restaurant.

Long established, large and usually crowded, there was most often a waiting line. There was no dessert on the menu and when you finished your meal, the waiters brought the check immediately, as they needed the table for the next in line. Despite this, we always had friendly and professional service. The place was remarkably consistent for many years.

But on one occasion, we had a waitress that we hadn't seen before. We ordered two lemonades and drank them. We were having our dinner and we ordered two more lemonades. They didn't come and they didn't come. We saw our busboy and asked if he could see to it that we got our lemonades, and he brought them promptly. After a while, our waitress came with the two drinks for us. She presented us with two lemonades, dripping with condensation on the outside of the glass, and they had a layered look. They had apparently sat for so long, the contents had started to separate. She could have at least stirred them or wiped them off to conceal the fact that she had forgotten them.

I told the waitress that the busboy had brought us some a little while ago, and she responded by asking, "What do you expect me to do with these?"

Well... I had an idea of what she could do with them, and my eyes betrayed me. My dining partner stopped me from verbalizing that idea by tapping me on the foot under the table. I expected the waitress to be polite, maybe even apologetic about forgetting our drinks. I can be forgiving. But she turned nasty, and put the two lemonades up on a shelf above our table where they dripped on us while we finished our dinner.

My dinner date asked me my professional opinion, and I said, "No tip." We never did see her again. The job was not for her.

In another instance, I was in the market for a lunch job. I saw an ad in the paper for 'waitress wanted' in a local café. The best way to see if you want to work in a new restaurant, is to go there and eat. So I asked my friend to join me.

We wandered in nonchalantly one afternoon to size the place up and sample the food and atmosphere. The restaurant was empty except for one woman sitting at a table, reading the newspaper. Apparently, she was the waitress. We seemed to be bothering her by asking for a menu. There were a few unusual items on the menu. I tried to engage her, partly to hear the description of the dish, but also to get a feel for her personality. After all, we were there checking out the place. Am I going to want to work here...with her?
She was very uninformative, essentially told us that everything

was self-explanatory and went back to reading her newspaper. She did bring us a rather forgettable lunch, but what was unforgettable was how rude she was. My verdict: "No tip."

I later found out that it was the owner who had waited on us! Needless to say, I didn't even apply.

❧❧❧

As a trainer of many new young waitresses and waiters, I often tell them not to worry about tips. They will come. In fact, the less you worry about them, the better it will be. Waiters who are only concerned about tips do not have their mind on their work, and it will be apparent. You have to make sure your work is done, keep the people happy, and pretend that it's you, yourself, sitting there in the restaurant. Also, it helps to love what you do, and let it show!

ANOTHER DAY-OFF INVITATION

Our next-door neighbors invited us over to their house for dinner. We literally climbed over the fence to share a meal outside on their picnic table. The neighbors had grilled some chicken, and we contributed by bringing a six-pack of dark beer and a pot of homemade spaghetti.

The evening was progressing smoothly until I made a *faux pas*. I was gesturing as I told one of my famous stories, and hit my bottle of beer, which spilled onto my plate. The beer gracefully flowed all around the edges, encircling my spaghetti.

I wasn't too concerned. My immediate thought was that beer could never ruin a good spaghetti sauce, as a solution to my problem occurred to me. I picked up my plate, gently tipping the overflow of beer into my mouth and then put the plate back down good as new.

I continued on with my story. As I looked over at our hosts, I realized that they were horrified. To this day, I don't know why. We were all adults at the table. It was a clumsy error, which I thought I had rectified. The hostess said, "I would never let my children do that!" It wasn't clear whether she meant tipping the plate, or drinking the beer!

The visit became progressively cooler, although it was a warm summer evening. We finished our meal and went home, never to return. The neighbors moved away shortly after that.

Was that really such bad etiquette? Drinking my beer off the plate? Remember it was a casual get-together, outside on a picnic table. After all, it was my dinner that got spilled on, and I stand by my solution to a rather insignificant problem. My actions should not have offended anyone, and given the same situation, I would do it again.

Table From Hell

My friends invited me for lunch at the restaurant where I worked at the time. There were four of us sitting in a cozy booth near the window. The boss brought over a plate of complimentary appetizers. It was fun to be there, and to be served by a co-worker.

Lunchtime was almost over, as we had stayed at the bar for a drink first, and the kitchen was about to close. My co-worker was anxious to take our order. I knew that the kitchen had a special dish, which they were preparing for dinner that night. It wasn't on the luncheon menu, but I asked if it was ready to be served and if I could have that. She looked annoyed but went into the kitchen to ask the Chef.

The Chef was reluctant, but agreed to make it for me. At that, two of my friends said that it sounded good and they would have it too! Since I worked there, they were following my lead. The fourth had a simple omelet, something actually offered on the menu. The waitress went back to tell the kitchen about the problem special order. Now there would be three! She didn't seem to be too happy with me.

Then things got worse. I have to stop gesturing when I tell my very funny stories, because this time I knocked over my water glass. Water and ice went everywhere.

What a mess! Remember, it was in a booth near a window. It wasn't easy to clean up. My co-worker, now very annoyed, had to clear the table, change the tablecloth and reset everything. The bell was ringing in the kitchen for her to come and pick up the special orders for our table. I knew that bell, and could hear its impatient toll.

The waitress and I had worked together for a few years, and she knew me well. She had heard me complain about 'Tables from Hell', customers who came in late, ordered items not on the menu, or had accidents that I had to clean up, making a change of tablecloth necessary. And here I was, being just such a customer, making not one, but all three of these *faux pas*. It meant much more work for my poor co-worker. My friends and I had become her Table from Hell.

Dripping sarcasm with every word, my co-worker facetiously asked, "Remind us again what it is that you do for a living?" I had to bow my head in acknowledgement and sheepishly answer, "I have no excuse, I'm a waitress."

EPILOGUE

When I was growing up, and all through high school and college, I swam competitively. My whole family was active in the sport, my three sisters and brother. When I was 14, my three sisters and I were the 'Fearsome Foursome' of a winning relay team. The rules for the relay team were one swimmer from each age group: 16, 14, 12 and 10. My sisters and I fit into the categories for one year only. We became locally famous by winning the county championship in Westchester County, New York in 1968! We received an inscribed plaque for the event.

After college, my brother and oldest sister kept up the swimming, mostly as exercise to keep in shape. I did not. I was busy watching people in restaurants and gathering experiences for later retelling.

Last fall, while I was writing this book, I received a phone call from my oldest sister. She said that she was beginning to train seriously with Masters Swimming in Connecticut. She had aspirations to qualify for the Nationals, which were being held here in California in May. My brother who has been actively competing for a few years, was her inspiration. I was to prepare myself. If she did qualify, she wanted to resurrect our family relay team.

Sure enough my sister swam fast enough to qualify, and I got the call, along with my other two sisters, that we were going to the Nationals! I hadn't been swimming competitively since 1975, when I graduated from college. I braced myself and joined my athletic club here and started swimming regularly. My brother had also qualified and was to swim in three events. We decided to make it a family affair...that's when we called our mother.

Mom had all those years ago supported us in our swimming habit: driving us to practice every day after school, driving to meets all over the locale every weekend, paying for all the pool memberships, gear and event entries, preparing delicious food for us with the proper carbohydrate content. She spent the long hours at the pool reading, knitting and officiating. She had to be there to witness this reunion. It was her 80th birthday, and the meet was to be held on Mothers Day. It was perfect.

We all went to the U.S. Masters Short Course Nationals, four days of events held in Clovis, and we girls swam in two relays. One freestyle, where all four of us swam the freestyle, and one medley relay, where we each swam different strokes. To add drama and style to the event, we wore flowered hats and Tina Turner glitter dresses. This caught the eye of the officials from *USMS Swimmer* magazine and we were featured in the July/August 2009 edition.

My mother sat in the bleachers for the four days of the meet, out in the hot sun. She was a trooper, keeping track of all events, telling us when it was our turn to 'warm up', and writing down all of our times, just like the old days. Our relay placed in the top twelve, but the reality of the five siblings swimming together, with our mom there, was like winning the gold.

We told anybody who would listen that we hadn't swum together like this for 41 years and that it was our mother's birthday! We had that old plaque inscribed with the new date 2009 and presented it to Mom.

During all these nostalgic and exciting festivities, I kept pulling out my manuscript saying "Read my book! Here, read my book!" My poor family was a captive audience. My mother was enthusiastic about my project and actually read most of it that weekend, which is quite a feat, considering all the hustle and commotion surrounding her. She was a teacher and knows syntax, grammar and styling. I watched her expression as she was reading. She smiled a lot which was reassuring, and finally said what I had been waiting to hear, "That's very nice, dear."

HI, I'M LINDA, I'LL BE YOUR WAITRESS TODAY

Have you heard the one about the woman who went into a restaurant...and stayed for 40 years! Well, that's me, and this book will help you understand why.

Let's face it. I didn't grow up dreaming about aprons, hairnets and comfortable shoes. I started waiting tables as part time summer employment while in high school. I found the work rewarding, although if someone had told me that I would still be doing this 40 years later, I would have said, "I have much better things to do with my life!"

But what could be better than meeting all kinds of interesting people and getting to know them. People come into restaurants for every sort of special occasion you can imagine, and I'm automatically included in whatever they're celebrating. Every day brings possibilities of adventure, meeting new folks and hearing tales of their lives.

When asked why I'm still here, my answer is, "They feed me, they pay me, and I don't really need a wardrobe." The same 'black and white' has suited me for many years.

Over the years I discovered that I'm actually in the entertainment business. My customers often share stories and jokes with me and in return I try to entertain them, and make their dining experience enjoyable and memorable.

When you come into a restaurant for a meal, it is the chef who provides the food. But it's the waitress you interact with, and it is the waitress who is privy to all the goings-on in the dining room. To discover just how entertaining these can be, read on...

"When people are eating, I'm working;
and fortunately someone's always eating!"

This book is dedicated to the men and women who have
chosen to become waiters, waitresses, servers and bartenders: working long hours, handling many different
circumstances while maintaining a positive attitude. This
dedication is in appreciation of your hard work to turn
the simple act of serving a meal into an art.

In Remembrance of:
Claude, Doris, Edgar, Mary,
Stretch, Jack and Charlie